THE AUTHENTIC LEADER AS SERVANT (ALS)

ALS I COURSE 8
REPRODUCTION LEADERSHIP
Attributes, Principles, and Practices

SYLVANUS N. WOSU, Ph.D

THE AUTHENTIC LEADER AS SERVANT
ALS I COURSE 8
Reproduction Leadership Attributes, Principles, and Practices

© Copyright 2024 by Sylvanus N. Wosu Ph.D.

Printed in the United States of America
ISBN: 979-8-9858816-8-4

All rights reserved. No part of this book may be reproduced or transmitted in any form or by any means, electronic or mechanical, including photocopying, recording, or by any information storage and retrieval system, without permission in writing from the copyright owner.

Bible quotations are from the New King James (NKJV) version of the Bible unless otherwise indicated.

Other versions used in this book are the New International Version (NIV), New Living Translation (NLT), King James Version (KJV), English Standard Version (ESV), and Good News Translation (GNT). Unless otherwise specified, NKJV should be assumed.

The views expressed in this work are solely those of the author and do not necessarily reflect the views of the publisher, and the publisher disclaims any responsibility for them.

To order additional copies of this book, contact:
Proisle Publishing Services LLC
39-67 58th Street, 1st floor
Woodside, NY 11377, USA
Phone: (+1 646-480-0129)
info@proislepublishing.com

PROISLE PUBLISHING

Table of Contents

FOREWORD — XI
ACKNOWLEDGMENTS — XV
DEDICATION — XVII
PREFACE — 19
   About Leader As Servant Leadership (LSL) Model — 22
   About the Authentic Leader as Servant (ALS) — 25
   About the ALS Courses — 26

CHAPTER 1
UNDERSTANDING LEADERSHIP ATTRIBUTES — 35
   Functional Definitions — 35
   Comparisons With Other Works — 40
   Principle of Leadership Attribute — 42
   Authentic Leadership Attributes — 43
   Summary 1 Understanding Leadership Process — 49

CHAPTER 2
LEADERSHIP REPRODUCTION ATTRIBUTE — 53
   Characteristics of Reproduction Attribute — 54
   Principle of Leadership Reproduction Attribute — 56
   Summary 2 Leadership Reproduction Attribute — 57

CHAPTER 3
DEVELOPING REPRODUCTION-SELECTION — 61
   Summary 3 Developing the Acts of Reproduction-Selection — 65

CHAPTER 4
DEVELOPING REPRODUCTION-MENTORING — 69
   Summary 4 Developing Reproduction-Mentoring — 77

CHAPTER 5
DEVELOPING REPRODUCTION-EQUIPPING — 81
   Summary 5 Developing Reproduction-Equipping — 85

CHAPTER 6
DEVELOPING REPRODUCTION- RELEASING — 87
   Summary 6 Developing Reproduction-Releasing — 93

TOPIC INDEX	97
REFERENCES	99

Foreword

The modern world today is obsessed with standardization and modalities. As a result, in the realm of leadership, many books have spout associated leadership theories and models and explain them as the path to follow. However, the critical dimensions that distinguish the effectiveness of any leadership process are the values and attribute the leader brings to the table; desired change is influenced by leadership styles or standards. These many standards and theories of leadership often are not in step with the changing times or the followers' needs. The trend is a bit like stocking different kinds of foods in a grocery store and expecting that they will meet everybody's needs the same way and at all times. Aisles are packed with varieties of food with expiration dates in the future, but getting the best deal on the products is what really matters to those who buy and use the products

In many ways, this is the state of leadership in the modern world. Increasingly, even leaders of public institutions are tasked with turning a profit for themselves or the organization they serve. The idea of a "leader" seems to float uneasily alongside the ranks of fundraisers or profit raisers in contrast to any kind of role model for followers or employees. That which is knowable, measurable, and marketable has surpassed the difficult intangibility of strong moral leadership attributes as the central guideline for achievement and success.

In this complicated space, Dr. Sylvanus Wosu introduces his complex idea of the Leader as a Servant Leadership, which is in this book, modeled on Christian tradition. Like all intricate ideas, Dr. Wosu's central point depends on a paradox: a person is best qualified to lead when he or she is most ready to serve. This paradox has been monopolized rhetorically by "public servants" who often serve either self-interest or the interests of specific lobbies. The Authentic Leader as Servant penetrates past the superficial concept of "serving" and details the internal state of true servitude or Servanthood.

While the book is primarily focused on the Christian model of leadership attributes such as discipleship, empathy, affection, and Servanthood, it does so not merely on the grounds of blind faith, but rather via numerous contemporary sociological and business-driven studies on how leaders should seek a leader-follower relationship that is simultaneously productive and nurturing. Dr. Wosu's most piercing insights always involve this secular–Christian dialogue. This book demonstrates that Christ's model for leadership is one that may exist successfully outside the confines of a faith relationship; it places the values of Christ's religious significance in leadership at the center of the framework. It is clear from Dr. Wosu's generous own life story of faith—a faith tested by humbling difficulties—is at the center of both his orientation and motivation for writing.

In language that is so concise, it is often illustrated in mathematical formulas; Dr. Wosu explains the deep structural integrity of Christ's Leader as the Servant Leadership model. One could imagine leaders of any doctrine benefiting from the analyses contained in these pages. The book's message repeatedly encourages the reader to imagine a scenario or reflect on memories and personal experiences to prove or test its many points. Thus, the book depends on a form of praxis, a lesson that could be or has been enacted, by the participating reader. I am very impressed at the volume and level of thinking of the author. Parts of the book involve his personal story, which is especially riveting. I cannot imagine what he had to endure, which he referred to as a" wilderness walk," to accomplish the goal he set for himself. His life stories on these pages are inspiring and stimulating.

In this way, the text eschews dogmatism in favor of the self-discovery Socratic Method of teaching and learning. The reader is not badgered into complying with a religious objective but is rather asked to consider the applicability of difficult biblical concepts in relation to modern life. It is a fascinating and very thought-provoking read.

Hence, the book does not seek to make the leader a servant, a cookie-cutter corporate buzzword, but rather asks the reader to imagine him or herself interacting with a range of concepts. One of Dr. Wosu's great strengths is his reservation when it comes to forcing his reading's interpretation on the material he presents.

The book parallels Biblical and modern leadership scenarios in ways that consistently provoke thought, and while it is clear Dr. Wosu has his particular leadership style; the space for the reader's own thoughts is always left open.

The book could not have been written in any other way with integrity. Its format and formulas are offered to the reader of the leader as a servant role that it analyzes in its pages. To find a text that instructs from this humble position is profoundly refreshing in a genre that is often packaged inside a cover with a sizeable picture of the "modest" author, smiling egotistically beneath a name spelled out in large, gold lettering. Throughout its pages, this text feels as if it serves the reader.

In the end, this is the most satisfying aspect of the book. There is no standardized approach to achieving successful leadership. There is no promise of power and a bigger payday; in fact, the book often proffers just the opposite. The reader is not encouraged to devalue the experience of leadership by finding some economic metric for marking success but is rather asked to think deeply about the most basic elements of internal and social interaction within the framework of a Christian tradition. What this means will be different for every reader. Indeed, even in the context of single chapters, I found myself questioning or re-evaluating moments of my own life. This book serves; it doesn't feel like filling in multiple-choice questions, staring at a wall of flavorless grocery products, or hearing the endless servant promises of today's political scene. It feels like a humble invitation to consider a single paradoxical element of a profoundly productive tradition.

-Tobias Bates

ACKNOWLEDGMENTS

A book on leadership attributes as aspects of Servant Leadership sprouted from the wealth of knowledge and the inspirations of many other leaders. Their writings were sources of inspiration, challenges, and examples of excellence to emulate.

Dr. Enefaa N. Wosu, my wife and life partner, for her love, commitment, and prayer support, especially during those long night hours I was not there for her and her constant reminder of who I must be as a leader-servant. Without her support, forbearance, wisdom, and encouragement, this project would not have been completed; I say, thank you very much.

And to God alone be all the glory and honor for the divine inspiration and guidance in initiating and completing this life-transforming book project.

DEDICATION

I humbly submit this book back unto the gracious hands of God who inspired the writings through His Holy Spirit!

I dedicate this book to my virtuous wife of 45 years, Rev. (Dr.) Enefaa Wosu whose spiritual leadership is an important gateway to our home, and to our four wonderful children—Prof. Eliada Wosu-Griffin EL, HeCareth, Tamuno-Emi, and Chidinma. From them all, I learnt what it meant to be a leader-servant. I could not be blessed with better teachers.

Preface

What characteristics did Biblical leaders like the Apostle Paul, Moses, Joshua, and Nehemiah as servants of their people display outwardly that distinguished them from other leaders, both then and now? The Apostle Paul kept his focus to *emulate* Christ and endured all the infirmities and persecutions he suffered to complete his goal to preach the gospel of Jesus Christ. He inspired Timothy and others through his effective *discipleship* leadership to imitate him as he emulated Christ. Moses' outward display of his *trust* in God's power earned him a good level of trust from the people and empowered him for the mission of delivery of God's children from bondage in Egypt; he had to *reproduce* himself in Joshua to complete the mission. But the greatest of them was Jesus Christ, who humbly sacrificed His life to finish the work of redemption. In His *Servanthood*, commitment, and love for the people, He became the ultimate *model* of a leader as a servant to *emulate*.

Let's consider for a moment secular leaders in these current times! For example, think of Henry Ford, who founded the successful Ford Motor Company; Bill Gates who created the global empire that is Microsoft; Albert Einstein, who in many ways is synonymous with a genius for his contributions to modern physics; Abraham Lincoln, remembered as one of the greatest presidents and leaders of United States; and many others like these we cannot mention. What did all these leaders have in common? What propelled them to turn their initial failures or challenges into eventual successes? None had a direct mentor or inherited any fortune from their parents. Nevertheless, they all eventually succeeded. These people can be distinguished from others based on their self-will to succeed, their self-confidence and belief in themselves, their self-determination, and their perseverance, among other characteristics. The distinguishing characteristics displayed externally in service or relationships toward others are the outward functional attributes that define that leader.

Think about yourself as a student, faculty member, or that new executive. What was it that made your journey to success different and even great? Students and colleagues, when they see or hear about my display of what I have referred to as the 'wilderness walk of faith', have asked me to share the critical attitudinal elements that made me remain inwardly resilient and undaunted and yet outwardly joyful in the difficulties I had faced. This book is the result of those reflections. Let me explain one such teaching moment.

Many years ago, sitting in my research lab on a Saturday morning trying to finish writing my dissertation, a fellow graduate student walked into the room to talk with me. He was contemplating terminating his graduate studies. He was a privileged single male student but felt the load was just too much.

"Sylvanus," he asked, with seriousness in his eyes, "your research advisor suggested that I should ask you, 'what is it that makes you tick?'.'What is it about you that makes you joyful and at peace with yourself and determined to finish, no matter the situations and high expectations we face in this department?"

What he asked me were deeply reflective questions, but I was willing and excited to answer them. Even so, before I do, let's look at the context. At that period in my life, I had four little children as a graduate student; in fact, more children than any of the faculties at that time, except for one faculty member who had eight children. I received little or no support from the department. I was then an international alien, did not qualify for financial aid, and was not given any research assistant position. I was, therefore, self-supported with two off-campus part-time jobs. I joked at being a minority of minorities, the only student in the department with such a label,—but I was self-willed to succeed. My adaptability attribute, coupled with perseverance and resilience, was all that I needed to succeed despite the odds against me. In every exam, homework assignment, or project I had to compete with students with full financial aid, plus they had nothing to distract their attention from their studies. I lived with the attitude that using disadvantages as an excuse was not an option. Aspiring to earn my Ph.D. was a life dream, and I was willing to give my ultimate best to actualize that dream even in the face of challenges. The choice was mine!

So I looked at my classmate and all I could see was a student striding through a valley through which I also walked. He needed me to show him how to walk the walk, to empathize with him. To answer his question, I smiled, not that I wanted to, but because it was just who I was. The joy he attributed to me was an overflow of my appreciation of God's grace that His life in me was externally manifesting His light to bless someone else. It was a great teaching moment; I capitalized on it to tell my classmate that my joy was not about me. He could see physically but about He who was in me, he could not see in the flesh; I needed him to know that I was just showing forth His life in me. At first, my classmate did not understand the spiritual prose or metaphor I was using. He looked surprised but open to hearing more.

I did not ask if he was a Christian. However, right on my desk was my small green pocket Bible. I opened to 2 Corinthians 12:9 (NIV) and handed it to him to read. As he read the passage: "But he said to me, 'My grace is sufficient for you, for my power is made perfect in weakness.' Therefore, I will boast all the more gladly about my weaknesses, so that Christ's power may rest on me," I noticed how absorbed he was in the words

He looked astonished and read it again, this time silently. "This is interesting, but what does this mean?" He asked. I took his question to mean, "How does this relate to my question?

I explained to my friend that the external attitudes he or my advisors saw in me that warranted the question, "What makes you tick" were inspired by my inner value system based on my faith in this same Christ and His teachings. My desire to manifest His life and self-confidence is all because of what He has promised in His word if I believed. I have believed His words and have gained self-determination and faith to make the right choices through Him for my life, and his spirit has given me perseverance and resilience to focus on finishing strong in pursuit of any goal. "With that faith, I have continued, more passionately and excitedly; I can look at my challenges and vulnerabilities and delight joyfully in them, even as an alien minority of minorities! His grace and power have empowered me to do all things I want to do. That is what makes me tick," I explained.

He looked at me as if he got his answer. "Wow, thanks!" he said, looking inspired and ready to face his challenges. As we concluded with a prayer, and he stood up to leave, I pointed empathetically to his face and said, "If I made it despite my challenges, you have absolutely no excuse but to persevere to complete your studies; you can make it too!"

It is fitting to report that this encounter with my classmate transformed his will and determination to continue. Yes, he was encouraged and went on to complete his graduate studies. He emulated self-will and perseverance from the example of the most vulnerable of all students in the department.

The inner value system of a Leader-Servant is founded not only on his faith but his self-will, coupled with self-leadership; it is the greatest mentor who can turn any situation into an inconceivable success. Self-will is the primary driver for determination, resilience, and perseverance. It is what wakes you up in the morning to ask for strength to do whatever it is you are setting out to do. Based on my life walk of faith, I can state with absolute certainty that faith is the unseen assuredness that can empower you to turn your life's probable impossibilities into great and improbable possibilities.

ABOUT LEADER AS SERVANT LEADERSHIP (LSL) MODEL

Looking at the testimony above, do you know the source that energizes the characteristics you display outside and how your inner self is related to what others see outside? What distinguishes you from others is what combines to define your attributes! As a follower, can you identify the characteristics that distinguish your leaders? As an executive, how do you base your evaluation of yourself? Or how do you evaluate that brand-new manager or new youth director you want to hire? To what do you compare the individual's qualities when you look at his CV? What is the basis of your measure? Do you know if you are a substantial leader? These personal questions and much more are the subjects of this two-volume book, 'The Authentic Leader as Servant Part I: The Outward Leadership Attributes, Principles, and Practices', is written in two parts; the second part 'The Leader as Servant Leadership Model. Part II'; deals with the Inner Strength Leadership Attributes, Principles, and Practices.

When we think about today's corporate greed, deepening divide between the haves and have-not, gridlock in political systems, conflicts and wars, high divorce rates, and the rich young ruler in the Bible, it is easy to agree that all these people share a few things in common: self-centeredness, pride, lack of compassion, and greed. There is a great need in today's suffering world for leader-servants who display leadership attributes. These attributes should be oriented toward selfless service to others. Indeed, our world is increasingly drifting away from global serving reality toward the self and apathy. The most credible message or model for a possible solution to this dilemma and the answer to several complex leadership questions can be found in the foundation of the ultimate leader-servant, Jesus Christ. This book defines the Leader as Servant Leadership attribute as the combined acts of two or more distinctive functional leadership characteristics exhibited in service and relationship toward others. There is no better time than now for a book that presents comprehensive and irrevocable facts and principles regarding how to develop effective attributes of the leader-servant.

The Leader as Servant Leadership Model

My first book on this subject, The Leader as Servant Leadership Model, explains that Jesus' servant leadership model is based on the notion of a Leader as a Servant and not on a Servant as Leader. There are four distinct differences between a Servant as Leader (Servant-leader) and the Leader as Servant (leader--servant) models. It is pertinent to highlight them here to connect to this book, Authentic Leader as Servant.

A Leader as Servant is a leader first. The leader–servant as a leader does not in the line of duty go projecting or lording his or her power and authority over others but is the person to lead the process of influencing desired changes in others through his humble example of being a servant or having a serviceable attitude toward others. He or she is a serving leader, not a lording leader. He leads as a servant by putting others' needs above his own needs and rights. Jesus emphasized the word "as" meaning that the leader (the Master) chooses to serve as a servant even though he is the leader. A leader–servant emulates Jesus, who gave up all rights, and emptied and expended Himself on His followers. He empowered them to become more like Him. A leader-servant is known as a leader first but is seen as a great leader by his humble attendant heart and acts of service to others. His greatness comes from his ability to put others above himself.

Leader as Servant is a Biblical Concept. The model or image of a humble serving leader motivated Jesus' disciples to see that if their master could do this for them, they must also be able to do it for others. Jesus clearly demonstrated the process of leader-as-servant leadership. In some cases, He chose to serve by leading when He wanted to create the image or model of the leader-servant in certain acts. In other cases, He chose to lead by serving, when he showed care and empathy toward the people and led the disciples to see empathy as a leadership attribute.

Leader as Servant is an Authentic Leadership Model to follow. The Leader as the Servant leadership model intentionally positions Jesus as an original model of a leader to follow.

He was serving His disciples to demonstrate that the process of becoming a great leader was earned through humble acts of service to others; He made them understand that He was empowering them to succeed Him as leader-servants through service to others. The result was an incomparable legacy of leadership that changed their communities. The fact that Jesus relinquished his rights or shared His power did not diminish His power and influence. In fact, his influence increased at least 11 X 100%, if we ignore the one case of Judas.

The Leader as Servant Transforms Organizational Culture. The proposed LSL model seeks to transform and sustain the community or organization by instilling key leadership values or "leadership presence" among followers or an organization's members. Change is sustained when everyone in the organization takes ownership of the change. Rather than focusing on leading more followers to be great followers who conform to the organizational culture, LSL seeks to lead and empower better leaders to be distinguished leaders and community builders.

There are four distinctions, which clearly differentiate many of the existing servants as Leader-based philosophies in relation to servant leadership from my LSL model. Even in the corporate or institutional worlds, there is nothing better than Jesus on which to base Servant Leadership. There is nothing more authentic and impacting than the servant leadership modeled by the life and teachings of Jesus Christ.

The LSL model uses exploratory questions, scenarios, and graphic visualizations to excite critical thinking in ways no other book on this subject has yet attempted. Several personal testimonies of my wilderness walk of faith with God are used to connect the reader to real-life experiences of the concepts discussed. The riveting effect is that the text engages and encourages the reader to walk through the experiences presented. The aim is to inspire the reader spiritually, mentally, and professionally with this far-reaching exposition on the subject of servant leadership.

About the Authentic Leader as Servant (ALS)

The *Authentic Leader as Servant* argues that no leadership model is as authentic, other-centered, able to build communities, and productive and service-oriented as the model of our ultimate leader-servant, Jesus Christ. No source can provide a better point of reference than that provided in the Bible. Hence, this book aims to be more than just a text on leadership; it hopes to be a personal discovery for those who aspire to develop effective leadership attributes that grow leaders as servants who ultimately develop thriving other-centered communities. This book presents a comprehensive, biblically-based study regarding how to develop these attributes and how they are applied in a servant leadership process. In this biblical context and for clarity, Servant Leadership means *Leader-as-Servant Leadership*. A *leader-servant* refers to a *leader as a servant*, which is distinct from a servant-leader or servant as leader.

Leader as Servant Leadership attributes are shaped by the Leadership's Inner Value system, which consists of character, motivation, and commitment. The *Authentic Leader as Servant* is presented as a necessary resource to complement my *The Leader as Servant Leadership (LSL) Model*. The LSL model integrates a transformative leadership framework and interactive dimensions of Servant Leadership. Leader as Servant Leadership is a process in which a leader, in his leadership position, purposefully chooses to put others' rights and needs above his positional rights and personal needs. He then serves, enables, and empowers followers for growth that builds a thriving organization. The LSL model looks at the predominant Servant Leadership concepts and shares how they compare with biblical principles on how we should lead and be led.

ABOUT THE ALS COURSES

The three books, *LSL Model* and *The Authentic Leader as Servant* (Parts I and II), together demonstrate that with today's global visions to reach people of all races and cultures, now is the time for an authentic servant's heart of service. Those visions and the leadership processes are most effective with the appropriate leadership attributes centered more on people than on the organization, principles regarding how to develop effective attributes of leader-servant.

The ALS I and II combined presented twenty leaders as servant leadership attributes. The series of ALS courses supply training guide to understand, develop, and practice the attributes in a leadership process. Each course is independent and self-contained and does not depend on completing any other course in the series of 20 courses. It is, however strongly recommended, in fact a must read, that chapters 1 and 2 in each series be covered as they lay the foundation of LSL model on which ALS is based.

ALS (Parts I & II) Course Layout

The *Authentic Leader as Servant (ALS)* leadership (parts I and II) book has been broken down into 20 courses in workbook format to achieve three goals 1) Self-discovery of the acts of developing the attribute under review in the course, 2) deeper understanding of the principles, research and biblical teaching behind the attributes, and 3) Learning the strategies for practicing the attributes.

Instruction

The set of questions following each chapter are designed to serve as a guide to discover, explore, and practice the essential ALS leadership attributes, principles, and practices in leadership process. The questions are comprehensive review based on the content of this specific chapter only.

To maximize the learning outcomes, the learner must read through this chapter and sections. Some referenced scriptures in the book are repeated in the summaries for added review if needed, even though they were discussed in the section in which they apply.

PREFACE

> The exercises that follow each chapter will help you in not only understanding your own strength and weaknesses in your acts of the attribute but will guide you in developing practical strategies you can apply in self-leadership process or helping others grow in leadership
>
> All answers to the questions are contained in the associated chapter or sections; consultation of new sources, except for the reference scriptures, is not needed. Thus, it is expected that you answer the questions after you have read the associated section or chapter of the workbook. The scripture or other references cited are only for references as they already discussed in the book

---

ALS I Course 1: Affection Leadership Attribute—*Affection flows from a person to produce positive emotions for the well-being of another person.*

An average person will define the word "love" in the sense that affection is a characteristic of love. Nevertheless, that definition clouds the functional meaning of affection as an attribute of a leader-servant. Affection is a love action intentionally given to someone to create favorable emotion. We experience a positive emotion when we receive or give affection. In his acts of affection, the Apostle Paul communicated to the Corinthian Christians how he spoke to them freely with an open heart, because it was an important way to give affection (2 Corinthians 6:11-13). He also spoke of longing for them with the affection of Jesus Christ (Philippians 1:8); an affection that needs to be mutual (1 Peter 1:7). How is the affection leadership attribute an outward leadership attribute? This course explores this and other questions to discover the characteristics of affection attributes and to formulate a functional principle based on the expected outcome of affection and the effective use of these attributes in leadership.

ALS I Course 2: Discipleship Leadership Attribute- *Discipleship transforms and empowers followers for service leadership that grows communities.*

Discipleship as an act of developing a follower toward a specific goal is an important function of leadership to equip others to lead. *Discipleship transforms and empowers followers for service leadership that grows communities*. A disciple is a follower who willingly chooses to follow the master and submits to his discipleship and authority. In that regard, Jesus wanted all his followers to be his disciples and ambassadors because a disciple is always a follower. Organizationally, a follower could be a junior employee, any employee in a brand-new department, a new younger faculty, or just any person that needs to be guided through a journey of professional growth and good success. This course focuses on the general growth of followers through the acts of discipleship and presents the critical characteristics of discipleship as a leadership outward attribute. Functional definitions of leadership discipleship attributes and its principle will be presented based on those characteristics. Each characteristic will be discussed in detail with emphasis on strategies of how they can be further developed or practiced as a part of the servant leadership process.

ALS I Course 3: Emulation Leadership Attribute—*A great leader-servant outwardly and positively inspires a pattern of good works for others to follow.*

To emulate is to strive to be like someone else or to follow someone else's example by imitating something that inspires you about that person. This course evaluates how to learn from someone good leadership qualities to develop yours. How did you use what you learned from following the footstep of your hero to grow your leadership qualities. Jesus in the scripture modeled humility and Servanthood he wanted his disciples to develop same qualities. Emulation as a leadership attribute shares some characteristics with transformative leadership, where a leader intentionally conveys a clear vision of a goal, inspires the passion for the work toward the goal, and motivates the followers to follow. As a leader, how do you model a characteristic behavior for someone to follow or develop? How is Leadership Emulation Leadership Attribute an outward leadership attribute? This course explores this and other questions to discover the characteristics of affection attributes and to formulate a functional principle based on the expected outcome of effective use of these attributes in leadership.

ALS I Course 4: Generosity Leadership Attribute: *Generosity is an outward measure of the level of sacrifice, what is shared, or the impact a giving makes, not just the size of the giving*

Generosity can be defined as "the *habit of giving* without expecting anything in return. It can involve offering time, assets, or talents to aid someone in need." Such habits can include spending your personal money, time, and/or labor for the welfare of others or expending (suffering or being consumed or spending) for others' well-being. When political leaders or Board members 'vote their conscience' on important issues that affect others, what is that "conscience" and how do such leaders contribute to the welfare of others? How can you, "Do all you can, with what you have, in the time you have, in the place where you are" for the betterment of humanity   All giving to help humanity is crucial to help meet the needs of the most vulnerable of God's children, as demonstrated by God as attribute of God, In this course, we will explore what distinguishes a leader's act of giving from his inside intentions. The key leadership characteristics of generosity will be discussed with respect to Servant-Leadership generosity Attributes and Principles and the details how a leader-servant can develop those characteristics and then effectively practice service leadership.

ALS I Course 5: Healing-Care Leadership Attribute: *Comforting others in any trouble with the comfort with which God comforts us, brings healing-wholeness*

What is healing Care and what does it mean in practical terms to you as a leader? Effective leadership begins with an emotionally and spiritually healthy leader who can reconcile and bring comfort to the followers, irrespective of followers' feelings (good or bad) toward the leader. The healing attribute and personal security complement each other. You must have the capacity for self-healing and individual security if you are to meet others' comforts. Personal security provides the infrastructure to support leaders in adversity and heal others that are hurting. A leader's or a group's success is measured by the strength of the weakest member or follower in the group or team… Healing is one of the most abstract and least understood attributes in leadership, and yet one of the most important. The key distinguishing characteristics will be explored to formulate a working definition and principle of leadership healing-care attributes based on those characteristics. Each characteristic will be discussed in detail with emphasis on strategies of how they can be further developed or practiced by a leader-servant as part of the servant leadership process.

ALS I Course 6: Influence Leadership Attribute-*The true measure of leadership success in affecting desired change in conduct, performance, and relational connections in others is influence*

Leadership is an integrative process in which a person applies appropriate (leadership) attributes to guide and influence the desired attitudinal changes in others toward accomplishing a particular goal. Eight five percent of CEOs of top companies surveyed on their climb to leadership ladder said they were "influenced by another leader," compared to 10% and 5% for "natural gifting" and "result of a crisis," respectively. When we consider influence as a servant leadership attribute, we are talking about a distinguishing leadership characteristic that displays on the outside what a leader is inside, influence takes on a deeper meaning. In this course, the key leadership characteristics of influence will be identified and explored from research to frame definitions of the Servant-Leadership influence attribute and principle. Based on those characteristics, the key outcomes of effective leadership influence 1 how a leader-servant can develop those characteristics and then effectively practice service leadership.

ALS I Course 7: Persuasion Leadership Attribute—*The means of transforming others to a new perspective is through empathetic persuasion.*

Persuasion attribute affords the leader the capacity to convince his followers or others to believe and engage in a new idea or goal through encouragement rather than using his positional authority or intimidation. Because members of the group may already have their views on an issue, the leader must carefully approach persuasion as a learning process to avoid conflicts or polarizing the group. He must unify the diversity of views to get buy-in and willingness to agree and follow. The leader-servant primarily relies on making decisions within an organization based on persuasion rather than positional authority. In other words, you will never hear the Leader-servant say, "Do it because I am the boss, and I say to." This particular element offers one of the clearest distinctions between the traditional authoritarian model of leadership and the concept of Servant leadership. In this course, we will explore the technique of convincing rather than coercing as one of the most effective ways a leader-servant can build consensus within groups. Key characteristics of persuasion leadership attribute will be found, fully discussed, and modeled from the examples in the lives of other leaders.

ALS I Course 8: Reproduction Leadership Attribute—*Great leaders produce successors for legacy and greater courses as an expected product of an effective leadership reproduction.*

In his book, *360 Degree Leader*, John C. Maxwell says, "Great leaders don't use people so they can win. They lead people so they can all lead together." Such great leaders, like Jesus, Moses, Paul, and others developed other leaders through a process of reproduction. Is it possible for leaders of today to reproduce their vision in others so that can lead and build a legacy together? The answer to this question is of course yes. However, the effectiveness of a leader duplicating his leadership qualities in a follower depends on the leadership reproduction attribute of the leader. This course explores the distinguishing characteristics of reproduction as an outward attribute in servant leadership. Functional definitions of leadership reproduction attribute and its principle will be presented based on those characteristics. Each characteristic of reproduction attributes will be discussed in detail with emphasis on strategies of how they can be further developed or practiced by a leader-servant as part of the servant leadership process.

ALS I Course 9: Servanthood Leadership Attribute— *A leader-servant is most qualified to lead when ready to serve as a servant for the growth of others.*

The last time you engaged in a practical act of service on the job, at home, church, or in your community, what were the key elements in that act of service? Did you serve because you wanted to and chose to serve? Or was it because someone asked you to? The ultimate goal is for the leader's life to positively transform many lives in his or her community of followers. Consider the New Testament teachings of Jesus, who demonstrated the ultimate Leader as Servant Leadership. Jesus equated greatness to serving unpretentiously (humbly, as would a child), and He equated leading with choosing to serve others. That is the first affirmative test of authenticity for this attribute. What were the distinguishing characteristics that enabled you to serve? How is the Leadership Servanthood an outward leadership attribute? This course will give answers and meanings to these and personal reflective questions to discover the distinguishing characteristics of The Leadership Servanthood attribute. Functional definitions of The Leadership Servanthood attribute and principle will be provided based on the identified characteristics. Readers will benefit from numerous techniques, personal examples, empirical case study, and applications of the concepts.

ALS I Course 10: Trust-Integrity Leadership Attribute—*True leadership trust produces assured trustee's confidence and readiness to follow based on the credibility, competence, and shared relational connections of the trusted.*

A study examined more than 75 key components of employee satisfaction in top leadership and found that trust and confidence was the single most reliable predictor of employee satisfaction in an organization. This course will examine the results of the above study with respect to servant leadership, and how a leader-servant increases the satisfaction of the followers in an organization. When the organization is going through some challenges, how can a leader be credible in helping the followers understand the company's mission and strategy? How can he share information on how the company or institution, or department is doing and how the followers or employees will be affected? Suppose the organization's strategy is not aligned with its inner value or character, how does the leader build trust in followers or earn trust from them? Organizational leadership trust has been defined by as "an employee's willingness to take a risk for a leader with the expectation that, in exchange, the leader will behave in some desired way." The course will examine how the element of reliance and confidence in the actions of the trusted and organization are characterized by a combination of Competence (Can they do the job?), Benevolence (Do they care about me?), and Integrity (Are they honest?).

Referenced Scriptures

A variety of Bible translations from over 11,200 original Hebrew, Aramaic, and Greek words to about 6,000 English words do exist with variations in meanings and emphases. I am not a biblical scholar and do not pretend to be one; Hence, I have avoided researching the roots of these words and personally prefer New King James Version (NKJV). I have intentionally used other translations for three main reasons; first, to allow for increased impact and alignment of words to the most desired meaning and emphasis in the concepts being addressed. Second, I wanted new and personal discovery of meanings from translations with which I have not been familiar. And third, I wanted to allow readers who may desire translations other than the NKJV the benefit of their preferred translations. Hence, in addition to the NKJV, other translations used in the book include New International Version (NIV), New Living Translation (NLT), King James Version (KJV), English Standard Version (ESV), and Good News Translation (GNT). Unless otherwise specified, NKJV should be assumed.

Sylvanus Nwakanma Wosu

CHAPTER 1
UNDERSTANDING LEADERSHIP ATTRIBUTES

Leadership attribute is the combined acts of two or more distinctive functional leadership characteristics exhibited in service and relationship toward others.

The starting point of our discussion is the understanding of the key functional definitions and concepts that describe the theme of this book. In general, I will define leadership as an integrative process in which a person applies appropriate attributes to guide and influence the sought-after attitudinal changes in others toward accomplishing a particular goal. Specifically, the Leader as Servant Leadership is a process in which a leader intentionally chooses to put the follower's rights and needs above his positional rights and personal needs, and serves, enables, and empowers them for desired spiritual and professional growth that builds thriving communities.

FUNCTIONAL DEFINITIONS

In the context of these definitions, I will begin the descriptions of the leadership attributes of an authentic leader-servant by offering a functional definition of Leadership Attributes, and showing how that definition differs from those of Leadership Character, Characteristics, and Traits.

Leadership Character is the sum total of personal qualities in leadership, such as honesty, values, vision, trust, and so on that make up the moral capital of the leader; Leadership character should describe who the leader is inside or the leader's basic personality traits.

The Leadership Characteristics describe the distinctive characteristics or features of a leader, such as attitudes, competencies, skills, and specific experiences that go beyond his character (personality). Leadership characteristics determine how (through skills and competencies) the leader leads or take actions in the process of leadership in any particular situation;

The Leadership traits are the distinguishing leadership characteristics of a leader (these are things that define his leadership characteristics), which differentiate from personality traits... Leadership traits are the set of characteristics that define a particular leader's leadership. This means that a leadership characteristic is a trait when it is a unique characteristic of the leader.

Leadership Attributes, unlike leadership character, characteristics, and traits, is *a leadership attribute and the combined act of two or more distinctive functional leadership characteristics exhibited in service and relationship toward others* or traits externally displayed in action toward others. All leadership attributes grow out of the leadership inner value system but can be externally displayed predominantly as an outbound or outward attribute or both:

1. **Outbound Attributes:** These are distinctive outward-bound attributes emanating from the inner strength of the leader to support external conduct in service and relationships toward others. They form the internal core functional qualities that motivate or enhance the outward manifestation of the inside character toward others. The outbound attribute such as listening and vision, for example, are the direct results of the inner values of the leader such as patience, hearing, love, humility, or all the fruits of the spirit.

2. **Outward Attributes:** These are distinctive functional outward outer visible attributes emanating from the richness of the outbound and inner values of the leader. For example, external attributes such as Servanthood, emulation/modeling, empathy, etc. are outflows from the leader who will directly impact the follower. Outward attributes can be enriched by the outbound (inner) attributes. As shown in Figure 1, the outward attributes in general form the outer core of

functional attributes in the leader as servant leadership, but they can share some overlapping functions with the outbound attributes.

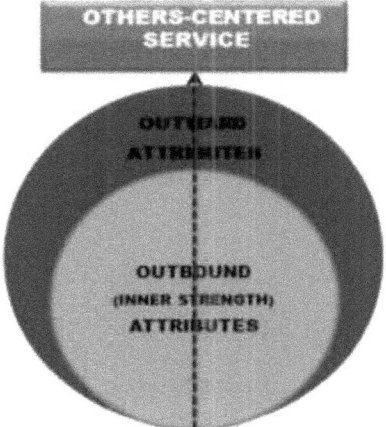

Figure 1.1. Servant leadership functional attributes

In summary, a leadership attribute is more than an ability or a characteristic; it is making those characteristics or abilities functional as part of how the leader acts (his habits) in service to others and applying those characteristics (beyond just having them) in personal and service relations to others. The character or known characteristic defines some aspects of your abilities or who you are inside— e.g. honest, humble, brave, etc. Your attribute, on the other hand, defines your habits; a display of how you use your characteristics, or the actions you exhibit toward others because of who you are inside. For example, empathy as a leadership characteristic becomes a leadership attribute if the followers can distinguish the leader's acts or habits of empathy, such as walking through with his followers in their state of suffering to bring wholeness; otherwise, it is just a characteristic or ability. Leadership attributes toward others are what impact the followers' and the organizational growth more than ability and competence.

In addressing one of the self-righteous hypocritical attributes of servitude leadership, Jesus called leader-servants to be "inside-out" leaders that reflect credibility; indeed, leaders should not appear outwardly righteous when they are full of hypocrisy and lawlessness in their hearts. He was describing "inside–out" as an authentic leadership attribute measured by the display of credibility a leadership attribute!

The measuring stick of a leader-servant is Jesus Christ. We measure ourselves unto the measure of the status of the fullness of Christ (Ephesians 4:13).

The leadership attributes of an authentic leader as a servant are encapsulated in **SERVANT/SERVING LEADERSHIP** are listed in Table 1.1, and defined in Table 1.2: *Servanthood, Emulation, Responsibility, Vision, Navigation, Adaptability, Trust, Listening, Empathy, Affection, Discipleship, Encouragement, Reproduction, Stewardship, Healing-Care, Initiation, Integrity,* and *Persuasion*. Other support attributes include *Influence, Courage, and Generosity*.

The attributes have been separated into Outward and Outbound (Inner Strength) leadership Attributes. As shown in Table 1.1, each of these attributes has three or more leadership characteristics. As such, more than 65 leadership characteristics are covered in these 20 attributes. For example, a leader's Servanthood leadership attribute is characterized by his willing servant's heart of selfless role humility, sacrifice, and submissiveness. The more these are present in a leader, the more effective the servant leadership.

Table 1.1: The functional leader-servant leadership Outbound (Inner Strength) and Outward attributes

	LEADER-SERVANT LEADERSHIP ATTRIBUTES			INNER STRENGTH ATTRIBUTES	OUTWARD ATTRIBUTES
S	Servanthood	L	Listening	Adaptability	Affection
E	Emulation	E	Empathy	Courage	Discipleship
R	Responsibility	A	Affection	Empathy	Emulation
V	Vision	D	Discipleship	Encouragement	Generosity
A	Adaptability	E	Encouragement	Initiation	Healing–Care
N	Navigation	R	Reproduction	Listening	Influence
T	Trust	S	Stewardship	Navigation	Persuasion
I	Influence	H	Healing–Care	Responsibility	Reproduction
G	Generosity	I	Initiation	Stewardship	Servanthood
C	Courage	P	Persuasion	Vision	Trust/Integrity

The list does not assume that a leader has to be excellent in all attributes or even have all of them to be an effective Leader–Servant. However, the more of these attributes the leader displays in his acts of service toward others, the more productive he or she will be, and the further his impact on the followers and organization. The table also shows that two or more attributes can share common characteristics, which can be applied or observed in different contexts. For example, a leader's ability to inspire followers can be seen in his acts of discipleship, empowerment, and encouragement attributes in the context in which these attributes apply. Each attribute is exhibited either as a part of the outbound inner strength attribute of a leader or a part of the outward attribute. Table 1.1 is not an exhaustive list of attributes; in fact, there are hundreds of such attributes. This is just the starting point.

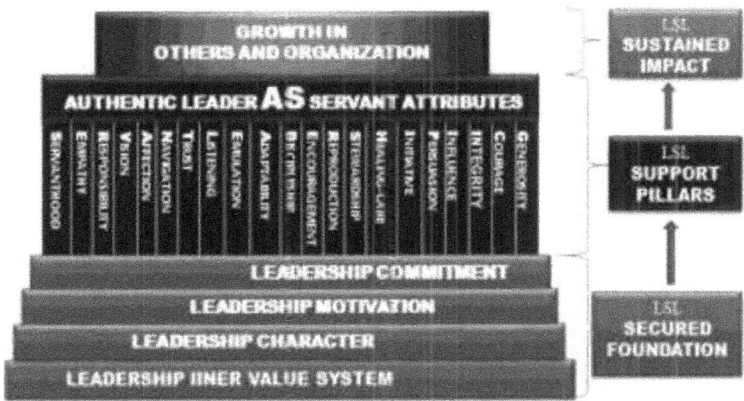

Figure 1.2: Servant leadership outward attributes (dark blue) and relationship to four foundational layers of the LSL Model

Figure 1.2 shows that the leader's attributes are shaped and secured by his four foundational layers (leadership inner value system, leadership character, motivation, and commitment). The attributes of the leader–servants are also conceptualized as the support pillars that will establish and support the personal authenticity of the leader, what the leader, does and the effectiveness of the leadership process. Thus, the attributes represent functional pillars of authentic leadership that can be learned or enriched as described in detail in the subsequent chapters. The combined effect of a secured foundation and stable support pillars will make a sustained impact on the growth of followers and the organization.

COMPARISONS WITH OTHER WORKS

The original works by Greenleaf (1970) in servant leadership [1] have been reviewed by Larry Spears (1996), who identified listening, empathy, healing, awareness, persuasion, conceptualization, foresight, stewardship, commitment to the growth of others, and building community as the ten distinguishing characteristics of servant leadership. [2] Russell (2001) has studied these attributes and have shown them to be essential in servant leadership and concluded that these qualities generally "grow out of the inner values and beliefs of individual leaders." [3] Russell and Stone (2002) extended the Greenleaf 10 attributes to 20 attributes observed in servant-leaders. These 20 attributes were categorized by these authors as either functional attributes (intrinsic characteristics of servant-leaders) or accompanying attributes (complement attributes that enhance the functional attributes).[4] The operational attributes were identified as vision, honesty, integrity, trust, modeling, service, pioneering, appreciation, and empowerment with the accompanying attributes of communication, credibility, competence, stewardship, visibility, influence, persuasion, listening, encouragement, teaching, and delegation. Only three of the attributes identified by Greenleaf were identified, and all three were accompanying attributes rather than functional. Responsibility, adaptability, affection, discipleship, navigation, and reproduction attributes which are considered critical in biblical-based servant leadership in my LSL model are not covered by Russell and Greenleaf. As shown in the description of the attributes in Table 1.2, most of the attributes reported by Russell and Stone (2002)[5] or Greenleaf [1] can be seen either in the twenty attributes or their associated characteristics. Integrity and honesty for example are leadership characteristics of trust and other attributes rather than an independent attributes. I take the position that servant leadership attributes are functional attributes in acts of duty to others and emanate from the inner value system of the leader.

CHAPTER 1
UNDERSTANDING LEADERSHIP ATTRIBUTES

Table 1.2: Description of the functional leader-servant outward leadership attributes and associated principles and characteristics

Leader–Servant Leadership Attributes	Principles of Leadership Attributes	Leadership Characteristics
Affection: *This is the combined love-based works toward providing the essential help or services for the spiritual growth or survival of another person. .* (Chapter 2)	*Affection flows from a person to produce positive emotions for the well-being of another person*	Kindness Compassion Practical Love Affective signs Appreciation
Discipleship: *This is the combined acts of personally developing, intentionally equipping, and attentively empowering growth in others to reproduce a heart of service.* (Chapter 3)	*Discipleship transforms and empowers followers for service leadership that grows communities.*	Inspiring Shepherding Equipping Developing Empowering
Emulation: *This is the combined acts of initiating an authentic servant attitude as a model of service worthy of following* (Chapter 4)	*A great leader-servant outwardly and positively inspires a pattern of good works for others to follow.*	Inspiration Motivation Initiation Model Following
Generosity: *This is the combined acts of freely sharing with and giving to others as an act of kindness, without expectation of reward or return to him.* (Chapter 5)	*Generosity is an outward measure of the level of sacrifice, what is shared, or the impact a giving makes, not just the size of the giving.*	Sharing Giving Kindness Affection Love
Healing-Care: *This is the combined acts of providing comfort and empathy to make others whole emotionally and spiritually along with tending to the follower's physical and mental well-being.* (Chapter 6)	*Comforting others in any trouble with the comfort with which we are comforted by God, brings healing - wholeness.*	Self-Healing Empathy Reconciliation Comfort Relational
Influence: *This is the combined acts of positively affecting desired change in conduct,*	*The true measure of leadership success in affecting*	Model Positive attitude Authority

41

performance, and relational connections toward others-centered course of action or service. (Chapter 7)	desired change in conduct, performance, and relational connections in others is influence	Connection Wisdom Intelligence,
Persuasion: *This is the combined acts of* communicating perspective to *connect, challenge, and convince with a compelling purpose to convert others to a new position.* (Chapter 8)	*The means of transforming others to a new perspective is through empathetic persuasion*	Connecting Challenging Communicating Convincing Converting Encouraging
Reproduction: *This is the combined acts of developing your leadership qualities in others and releasing them as successors to continue a greater mission.* (Chapter 9)	*Great leaders produce successors for legacy and greater courses as an expected product of an effective leadership reproduction.*	Selecting Mentoring Equipping Empowering Releasing
Servanthood: *This is the combined acts of humility, willingness, and intentionality in service to others through selfless sacrifice and submission as a servant.* (Chapter 10)	*A leader-servant is most qualified to lead when most ready to serve as a servant for the growth of others. The role of a leader is to serve as a servant*	Servant's heart Humility Sacrifice Service Willingness Submissiveness
Trust: *This is the combined acts of positive display of character, competence, credibility, and shared relational connections that produce assured trust-confidence of the trustee in the trusted.* (Chapter 11)	*True leadership trust produces assured trustee's confidence and readiness to follow based on the credibility, competence, and shared relational connections of the trusted.*	Character Competence Integrity Credibility Confidence

PRINCIPLE OF LEADERSHIP ATTRIBUTE

In the context of servant leadership, a leadership attribute is a level above the leadership characteristic or trait of a leader. The principle of leadership attribute states that every leadership attribute has a set of distinguishing characteristics that make up the inward or outward display of the attribute. The principle reflects the essential designed purpose or outcome of the attribute or the inevitable consequence of the effective practice of the attribute. Thus, the principle of leadership attribute is a concise statement about the fundamental truth, value, or belief about the attribute in a leadership situation; it is a statement that establishes an idea about the outcome of the attribute for guiding the practical application of the attribute and its characteristics. I will postulate and frame each principle as an additive function of the characteristics of the attribute. A statement of each principle is quoted at the beginning or below the title of each chapter. It is yet to be experimentally proven if the attribute is a linear or some other non-linear function of these characteristics as variables. It is expected, however, that each character will contribute to the effectiveness of the attribute in varying degrees.

AUTHENTIC LEADERSHIP ATTRIBUTES

At a personal level, attributes are the value-based inside-out moral leadership assets that can be related to the authenticity of a leader-servant. The complexity of defining authenticity has been noted in the literature. The subject of authentic leadership is well covered in the works of Terry (1993),[5] George (2003),[6] and Shair and Eilam (2005).[7] All appear to agree that authenticity requires self-awareness and objective self-identity in personal and social interactions with others. In his book, *Advocacy Leadership*, Professor Gary L. Anderson offers individual, organizational, and societal perspectives on authenticity: "Authenticity, at a peculiar level, is living a life, whether in the private or professional term. This is congruent with one's espoused values; at the structural level, authenticity has to do with viewing human beings as ends in themselves, rather than means to other ends; at the public level, it is a state of affairs that is congruous with the shared political and cultural values of society."[8]

The basic tenets of these perspectives are very fitting to authenticity as a qualifying element of leader-servant leadership attributes. The attribute reflects how the followers see the leader based on the leader's distinctive features displayed through his or her actions personally, organizationally, and societally. The leader is seen as a leader-servant or serving leader because the followers see him lead as a servant from an inside-out value of others. This is what makes the leader authentic. Authenticity means that what a leader displays outside, in personal or leadership life of service to others, and society is based on the values the leader espouses inside.

Authenticity in servant leadership can be one or two types or both: *Outbound Authenticity and Outward Authenticity*: The Outbound (outward-bound) Authenticity is the genuineness of personal honesty from your inner strength and abilities; what you say and how you act emanate from who you are or how you feel inside. It reflects the essential truth and honesty about your outward-bound inner strength.

Outward authenticity, on the other hand, describes the truthfulness of your credibility and honesty displayed outward in relation to others; your *outer* visible behavior or how you act outwardly towards others reflects exactly your true intentions.

While *outward* authenticity is the visible *outer* indicator of the truth of who you are inside, *outbound* authenticity is outward-bound attribute from the inside of who you are. Credibility in this context is the influence a leader has to attract believability, trustworthiness, and authenticity; it is the believability, trustworthiness, and authenticity of who you are inside and outside.

A key element of personal authenticity is that it is seen or measured in the context of societal, cultural, and organizational interactions. In that context, achieving individual authenticity becomes a challenge since it is influenced by social factors and dispositions of individuals who usually depend on liberal and organizational realities. However, for leader-servant leadership, the leader can face those changing times by remaining focused on his key Biblical-based principles or *Leadership Inner Value System*. Thus, I am interested in authenticity as an essential element of effective Leader-servant leadership attributes or Leader-servant leadership attributes as drivers of leadership authenticity. With that in mind, the first critical element of authenticity in practicing or developing efficient leader-servant leadership attributes is inside-out self-examination relative to the people served rather than the organization. You may ask yourself: What will be my response when the people I lead act or react in a certain way, will it be negative or positive? What are my strengths and vulnerabilities at those times?

CHAPTER 1
UNDERSTANDING LEADERSHIP ATTRIBUTES

Professor Yacobi in his post, "Elements of Human Authenticity," noted that since "the self-arise attribute emerges from interactions between self, others, and the environment in a complex society and world, there may co-exist multiple complicated identities depending on place and context." [9] He went on to identify the following <u>essential elements of personal authenticity</u>: self-awareness, unbiased self-examination, accurate self-knowledge, reflective judgment, personal responsibility, and integrity, genuineness, and humility, empathy for others, understanding of others, optimal utilization of feedback from others. All of these are covered under the leadership attributes or characteristics shown in Table 1.2.

Bill George, in his book, *Authentic Leadership*, takes the position that to be an authentic leader; a person must have the following essential characteristics: [10]

- Behavior based on value: He must understand his own values and exhibit behavior to others based on those values;
- He must not compromise his values in difficult situations but could use the situation to strengthen personal values in those situations.
- Passion from a clear purpose: Be self-aware of who he is, where he is going, and the right thing to do.
- Compassion from the heart: He must lead from a compassionate heart that allows them to be sensitive to the plight and needs of others,
- Connectedness from a relationship; he must be relationally connected with people he leads.
- Consistency from the self-disciple He must demonstrate self-discipline to remain calm, collected, and consistent in a stressful situation.

Modeled after the elements above, Table 1.3 lists six essential characteristics of authenticity for servant leadership. These fundamental characteristics cover the five identified above and can also be aligned with the leadership characteristics in Table 1.2. Each attribute in Table 1.2 is expected to pass the personal authenticity test in Tables 1.3, 1.4. In a survey of 132 Christian leaders, seventy-four percent (74%) of them agreed that they always or frequently exhibit servant leadership attributes. [11] Thus, a pass of the outward authenticity test means that a pure leader must demonstrate 70% or more of these essential elements of this legitimacy. (That is, 70% YES in the assessment questions in Tables 1.3, 1.4).

It needs to be noted, however, that a secular leader could be authentic and still lack some of the essential servant leadership attributes or characteristics such as selflessness, servanthood, and love-motivated servant attitudes of a leader-servant. Effective leader-servants are authentic leaders and personal authenticity is an essential element of leader-servant leadership. The key test for leader-servant authenticity is the quality of his inside-out value and personal character. What is most important is a change from the inside-out.

	Table 1.3: The test of essential elements of personal inner strength authenticity in servant leadership		
	Elements of Inner Strength Authenticity	**Inner Strength (Outbound) Authenticity Assessment Questions**	**YES / NO**
1	Personal inside-out value-based behavior	Are your personal inside-out values aligned with acts of service and behavior outside?	1
		Are you honest to yourself in relation to your inner strengths and abilities?	2
2	Inside-out Self-Awareness	Do you have unbiased self-examination, and accurate self-knowledge of who you are inside-out?	3
		Do you know your inner strength and weaknesses in relation to the good you want to show as an outward attribute?	4
3	Inside-out Empathy-Compassion	Do you know and feel from your inside what you want for your followers?	5
		Are you motivated to empathize, based on your inside feelings?	6
4	Inside-out Connection with followers	Do you feel deep, personal, and spiritual connection with your followers?	7
		Does what you say and how you act reflect how you feel when you relate to others?	8
5	Inside-out Emotional Self-regulation	Do you have difficulty controlling your emotion in order to remain calm in a stressful situation?	9
		Are you always able to comfort yourself?	10
6	Inside-out Authenticity Feedback	Do your followers see your inside-out value from your outside behavior?	11
		Will your followers feel that what you say you are is congruent with how you act?	12
	#YESs_____ ; # NOs_____ : Outbound Authenticity: YES/ 12————%		

Chapter 1
Understanding Leadership Attributes

Table 1.4: The test of essential elements of personal outward authenticity in servant leadership

	Elements of Personal Outward Authenticity	Personal Outward Authenticity Assessment Questions	YES or NO
1	Personal value-based outward behavior	Are your personal values and beliefs aligned with your acts of service and behavior toward others?	1
		Do you live out your life according to your beliefs?	2
2	Personal Self-Awareness	Do you have clarity of your personal vision and purpose?	3
		Does what you know about yourself accurately describe what others say?	4
3	Personal Outward Empathy-Compassion	Do you apply how you feel to what your followers need?	5
		Do you lead from a compassionate heart and are you sensitive to the plight and needs of others?	6
4	Personal Connection with followers	Do you feel deep, personal connection with your followers?	7
		Does your outward action toward others reflect exactly your true intentions?	8
5	Outward Emotional Self-regulation	Do you have difficulty controlling your emotions to remain calm in a stressful situation?	9
		Does your evaluation of your value of others agree with how valued they feel?	10
6	Personal Authenticity Feedback	Do your followers see your outward acts as true and honest?	11
		Can your followers see other-centeredness in 70% or more of your attributes?	12

#YESs_____; # NOs_____; Outward Authenticity: YES/ 12 _____ %

ALS REPRODUCTION LEADERSHIP
ATTRIBUTES, PRINCIPLES, & PRACTICES

Table 1.5. Leader As Servant-Leadership Audit						
A servant-leader in his leadership position purposefully choses to serve and inspire acts of service in others by his example. Select and circle best answer to questions 1=Never: 2=Almost never ; 3=Sometimes; 4=Frequently; 5 =Always						
	Servant Leadership assessment questions	Circle no				
1	I am willing and other-centered, and readily chose to serve others as a servant for their personal growth	1	2	3	4	5
2	I model others-centered attitude in my service and relationships and inspire same for others to follow	1	2	3	4	5
3	I have a sense of obligation, willingness, and accountability for the service towards others	1	2	3	4	5
4	I have the foresightedness to specify in the present view what others' growth should be in a given future	1	2	3	4	5
5	I work toward providing the essential help or services for the spiritual growth or survival of the others;	1	2	3	4	5
6	I provide the needed purposeful course of action for how to chart the course to for my followers.	1	2	3	4	5
7	I display external credibility and a strong sense of character based on values, beliefs, and competence;	1	2	3	4	5
8	In communication, I attentively perceive and hear what is communicated, reflectively listen to understand and to be understood	1	2	3	4	5
9	I walk through with others in their state (suffering, emotions, etc.) in a way that provides the needed care and well-being	1	2	3	4	5
10	I have a measure of self-secured flexibility to adapt appropriate attitude to serve all people in different situations	1	2	3	4	5
11	I personally develop, intentionally equip, and attentively nurture spiritually growth in others	1	2	3	4	5
12	My act of bravery instills in others the courage and confidence to follow or persevere in a course of action	1	2		4	5
13	I develop my leadership qualities in others as successors to continue in a purposeful mission	1	2	3	4	5
14	I manage , maintain,, and account for all resources entrusted to me and being responsible for the difference my acts make	1	2	3	4	5
15	As a care-giver, I act to comfort and make others whole emotionally	1	2	3	4	5
16	When I see a need, I originate a vision and action, and stay committed to meet that need and desired change	1	2	3	4	5

17	I display a holistic view of an issue to inform, transform or convert others to my view through empathetic persuasion	1	2	3	4	5
18	I freely share what I have sacrificially as an act of kindness to others, without expectation of reward in return	1	2	3	4	5
19	My act of influence is to affect the actions, behavior, opinions, etc., of others based on trust, credibility and relationship	1	2	3	4	5
20	In the face challenges and danger, I act with bravery to overcome fear and take a stand with strength and conviction	1	2	3	4	5
Score Range	Add up the numbers in each column (Total Score____) Check and Understand the key areas to work on					
81-100	Strong Leader-Servant; keep it up, go and train others.					
66-80	Above average Leader-Servant; work 25% of key areas					
50-65	Average but developing; need to work on 50% of key areas					
34-49	Below average leader; work on 75% of key areas					
<34	Not a Leader-Servant; need training in all areas					

SUMMARY 1
UNDERSTANDING LEADERSHIP PROCESS

Before starting this exercise, please read and follow the instruction in the preface of this workbook. Answers to these questions are contained in this chapter. Completion of these exercises after reading the chapter should take 60-90 minutes.

Discovering the Leadership Attributes

1. What is your alternative definition of leadership? In learning to lead, how would you differentiate the following elements:
    a. Leadership,
    b. Leader as servant leadership.
    c. Leadership characteristics.
    d. Leadership attributes
2. How should you lead in the context of this chapter?

Understanding the Leadership Principles

1. Define or state the principle of Servanthood Leadership attribute. How true is that in your leadership experience?
2. What are the key differences between the Leader as Servant and the Servant as Leader Leadership philosophies?
3. How can you display the essential qualities of authentic leader in a leadership process in challenging times.?
4. What are the characteristics of a leader-servant?
5. What was the original source of the Servant as Leader (SL)? What was the original source of Leader as Servant (LS)?
6. How do you compare the two model characters of Leo in SL and Jesus in LS
7. What is the key framework of a Leader as a Servant Leadership?

Practicing Authentic Leadership

1. Authenticity in servant leadership can be one or two types or both *Outbound Authenticity and Outward Authenticity*: Describe a time when you displayed:
    a. The Outbound (outward-bound)— *outbound* authenticity is outward-bound attribute from the inside of who you are.
    b. *The Outward Authenticity*—*outward* authenticity is the visible *outer* indicator of the truth of who you are inside,
2. Describe the key elements of personal authenticity seen or measured in the context of societal, cultural, and organizational interactions.
3. Take the outbound (Table 1.3) and Outward (Table 1.4) leadership authenticity tests. How (%) authentic are you (#YES/12) in each measure in your leadership process?
4. In the elements you rated as NO, review the relevant passage, learn what is missing in you and write a personal commitment statement on how to work to improve in those areas
5. How much of a leader-servant are you? Take the personal leader-servant audit in Table 1.5 to self-assess your effectiveness.
6. Based on the questions in Table 1.5, can you identify each of the twenty attributes? What ones did you score 3 ("sometimes") or less than 3? Review and learn and commit to work to improve.

CHAPTER 2
LEADERSHIP REPRODUCTION ATTRIBUTE

Great leaders produce successors for legacy and greater courses as an expected product of an effective leadership reproduction

In his book, *360 Degree Leader*, John C. Maxwell says, "Great leaders don't use people so they can win. They lead people so they can all lead together." [40] Such great leaders, like Jesus, Moses, Paul, and others developed other leaders through a process of reproduction. Is it possible for leaders of today to reproduce their vision in others so that can lead and build a legacy together? The answer to that question is of course yes. However, the effectiveness of a leader duplicating his leadership qualities in a follower depends on the leadership reproduction attribute of the leader. This chapter explores the distinguishing characteristics of reproduction as an outward attribute in servant leadership. Functional definitions of leadership reproduction attribute and its principle will be presented based on those characteristics. Each characteristic of reproduction attributes will be discussed in detail with emphasis on strategies of how they can be further developed or practiced by a leader-servant as part of the servant leadership process.

CHARACTERISTICS OF REPRODUCTION ATTRIBUTE

One of the best examples of multiplication other than Jesus Christ reproducing Himself and ministry in the disciples was the Apostle Paul's mentoring and training of Timothy for church growth. Mentoring or training for reproduction requires careful selection of potential leaders or mentees. As a great leader whose mission was to spread the Gospel, Paul's recommendations to Timothy (1Timothy 5:17-22) for established leaders in the church including the following steps:

(1) Identify and select those with character, gifts, and Influence.
(2) Separate and set them apart for the work of their calling;
(3) Prepare and equip them with the tools and experiences they need;
(4) Recognize them publicly to affirm their calling to the church;
(5) Honor those who serve well; and
(6) Ordain and anoint them by laying on of hands and commissioning them for the work.

These recommendations flow out of Paul's particular leadership qualities. He was, in essence, giving to Timothy what has worked well in his own practice.

Another example that shows the direct impact of reproduction was the reproduction leadership style of Moses. Before becoming a great leader, Moses was a great servant, single-handedly judging Israel "from morning until evening" and getting worn out in the process. In observing this method of leading the people, Moses' father-in-law Jethro advised him in Exodus to select, train, and release a few people to help him: "... You shall select from all the people able men, such as fear God, men of truth... then it will be that every great matter they shall bring to you, but every small matter, they shall judge" (Exodus 18:18-22).

Obviously, Moses' father-in-law Jethro observed that Moses could do better if only he could reproduce himself on some few people. So, what characteristics did Moses display to produce other leaders and change from his ministering and judging to leading? Jethro's advice was for Moses to reproduce his leadership qualities in others so that instead of mediating all the people by himself, he needed to lead others to judge by standing before God for the people (praying), training, commissioning, releasing, and guiding other leaders to lead according to their abilities. Moses took the following six strategic actions:

(1) **Connect them to God**: He presented the people and their challenges before God;
(2) **Select and develop able men**: He selected able men (non-covetous men of truth that fear God) and developed them as leaders;
(3) **Teach them God's Law**: He taught the people the status and laws of God.
(4) **Communicate the vision and mission**: He developed and communicated the vision, plan, and the way they must walk, their specific responsibilities, and his expectations;
(5) **Commission the trained men as heads**: He commissioned them as heads over people and with a direct connection to them;
(6) **Release the heads to do and manage the work**: He released them to do the work according to their abilities.

Which of these strategies is distinctive in producing the successor of a leader-servant? To see the key dimensions of reproduction that establish a lasting legacy for a leader-servant, we see again the way Moses, the servant of God, reproduced himself in Joshua:

> *"Then Moses spoke to the LORD, saying: "Let the LORD, the God of the spirits of all flesh, set a man over the congregation, who may go out before them and go in before them, who may lead them out and bring them in, that the congregation of the LORD may not be like sheep which have no shepherd." And the LORD said to Moses: "Take Joshua the son of Nun with you... And you shall give some of your authority to him... At his word, they shall go out, and at his word, they shall come in, he and all the children of Israel with him—all the congregation." Numbers 27:18-23*

Moses was thinking of a person who will be able to do what he (Moses) does. Note what Moses considered to be the most important part of his act of leadership of the congregation. They include the ability to:

- Be over the congregation,
- Lead in front and lead from behind,

- Lead from within,
- Guide them out and in, and
- Be a shepherd.

Moses' strategies to reproduce the above qualities can be identified from the instructions God gave to him. Moses was to:

- Select a Spirit-filled man like Joshua,
- Equip him spiritually by anointing by laying of hand;
- Set him apart to commission him,
- Set and affirm him openly,
- Inaugurate him publicly to empower him
- Release him with authority.

These instructions contain most of the key dimensions needed for Moses to reproduce the leadership qualities he wanted and requested in Joshua as his follower or mentee. This follower will be a new leader who will complete the task of leading the people or congregation toward an established goal or vision. In this case, the goal was to lead the people to the Promised Land.

PRINCIPLE OF LEADERSHIP REPRODUCTION ATTRIBUTE

The aforementioned examples from Moses, Jesus, Paul, and other biblical leaders provide several lessons to learn how leaders can reproduce themselves in others or simply develop other leaders toward a desired vision. The key distinguishing leadership characteristics from the above examples are *Selection, Mentoring, Equipping, Empowering, and Releasing*. Since selecting, mentoring, equipping, and empowering are all stages of developing the desired leadership qualities, my working definition is presented as follows:

> *Servant leadership reproduction attribute is the combined acts of developing his or her leadership qualities in others and releasing them as successors to continue a greater mission.*

CHAPTER 2
LEADERSHIP REPRODUCTION ATTRIBUTE

The primary result of effective reproduction attribute is the production of Leadership successors and legacy. The legacy is passed on by releasing the new leader with the responsibility to multiply and reproduce others to lead by serving. This principle is stated as follows:

Servant leadership reproduction principle: Great leaders produce successors for legacy and greater courses as an expected product of an effective leadership reproduction

The reproduction attribute is externally displayed through the leader's acts of selecting, mentoring, growing, equipping, and releasing. This is illustrated in Figure 9 and expressed as:

SELECTION + MENTORING + EQUIPPING + RELEASING = REPRODUCTION

How do these characteristics of reproduction establish leadership and a successor of a leader-servant? What are the attributes you want to model for a follower or see displayed by a follower? As professors, how do you select graduate students you want to reproduce as experts in your field or will be a good apprentices for your research? Answers to these questions are explored for each of the characteristics above.

SUMMARY 2
LEADERSHIP REPRODUCTION ATTRIBUTE

Before starting this exercise, please read and follow the instruction in the preface of this workbook. Answers to these questions are contained in this chapter. Completion of these exercises after reading the chapter should take 60-90 minutes.

Discovering the Reproduction Leadership Attribute
1. What is reproduction leadership attribute?
2. How can a leader reproduce their vision in others so that can lead and build a legacy together?

ALS Reproduction Leadership
Attributes, Principles, & Practices

3. What are the distinguishing characteristics of reproduction as an outward attribute in servant leadership? Functional definitions of leadership reproduction
4. How did Jesus demonstrate multiplication principle
5. What can we learn from Paul's recommendations to Timothy (1Timothy 5:17-22) for established leaders in the church
6. How did Moses shows the direct impact of reproduction" (Exodus 18:18-22).
7. What six steps did Moses take to reproduce his leadership qualities in others?
8. Which of these strategies is distinctive in producing the successor of a leader-servant?
9. How did Moses reproduce himself in Joshua to establish a lasting legacy, see *Numbers 27:18-23*
10. Moses was thinking of a person who will be able to do what he (Moses) does. What did Moses consider to be the most important part of his act of leadership

Practicing the Act of Reproduction Attribute

1. Moses' strategies to reproduce the above qualities can be identified from the instructions God gave to him. Fill in the blanks: Moses was to:
   a. _____ a Spirit-filled man like Joshua,
   b. _____ him spiritually by anointing by laying of hand;
   c. Set him apart to _____ him,
   d. Set and affirm him _____,
   e. Inaugurate him publicly to _____ him
   f. _____ him with authority.
2. How do these characteristics of reproduction establish leadership and a successor of a leader-servant?
3. What are the attributes you want to model for a follower or see displayed by a follower?
4. As professors, how do you select graduate students you want to reproduce as experts in your field or will be a good apprentice for your research?

CHAPTER 2
LEADERSHIP REPRODUCTION ATTRIBUTE

Understanding the Principle of Leadership Reproduction Attribute

1. Since selecting, mentoring, equipping, and empowering are all stages of developing the desired leadership qualities, how do you define Servant *leadership reproduction attribute,* what is the primary result of effective reproduction attribute.
2. State the principle of Reproduction Leadership Attribute
3. State the additive law of reproduction attribute

Practicing Reproduction-Attribute (Ch. 9)

1. What would you consider the key characteristics of reproduction leadership attributes?
2. How many acts of reproduction as an attribute do you display?

CHAPTER 3
DEVELOPING REPRODUCTION-SELECTION

A good reproduction -the selection process is the starting point of reproduction. Reproduction–selection attitude is the leader's competence in choosing the correct candidate to be developed as a successor.

Selection could also mean modeling the attribute that your followers will want to emulate or attracting the right candidates to yourself. The selection process involves the following four essential elements: Identifying the potential leaders, assessing longed-for character and competency that need to be trained, assessing teachable habits that will encourage desired submission for growth, and the mentee accepting and committing to becoming like the mentor. The subsequent strategies can strengthen a mentor's competence for reproduction–selection:

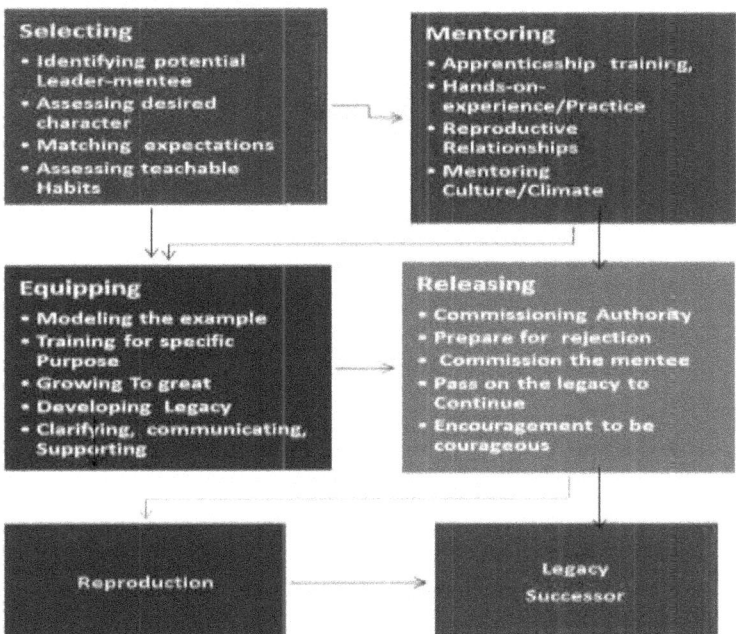

Figure 9: Four-stage progression process model of servant leadership reproduction-attribute.

Identify mentee as a potential successor

The beginning process in leadership reproduction- the selection is the ability to identify and hand-picked a candidate with the minimum qualifications based on certain factors and who also possesses talents such as character, experience, convictions, and a relationship with the leader. This is one of the critical elements of leadership—the ability to select the right people with the character and basic qualifications that can further be trained for the specific job. Selecting the candidate also requires understanding and matching the leadership tasks and expectations with the candidate's minimum qualifications or abilities. What did God see in Moses that made Him insist on convincing Moses to initiate the exodus of the Children of Israel out of Egypt? God wanted a patient diplomat who will be submissive to His leadership. Moses moved from being a one-person ministering judge to a leader-servant delegating according to the gifts he saw among the people. Followers included Joshua, Elisha, the Apostles, Timothy, Paul, and others like them. What can we learn from their growth as leaders?

Assess desired character and competency

Assess the desired character and competency that need to be trained. This is essential for a matching character to the expectations of the office. Moses demonstrated a good example of selecting Joshua as his successor (Numbers 27:17-23). Moses asked the Lord to identify and set a man over the congregation who will be able to lead and guide them in and out. He presented his understanding or definition of what leadership was—the act of leading and shepherding people in all aspects of their lives. Moses knew who he was and what this fresh leader needed to lead the congregation effectively into the Promised Land. He compared Israel to sheep—not knowing where to go, and he saw the leader as a shepherd that must be able to care for the sheep and lead them out to pasture and into a new land. He knew and sensed the dangers ahead, the wars that needed to be won, and the land that needed to be possessed. Moses also knew that God is the Spirit of all flesh and knew the best man for the job. And God immediately responded to Moses' request and helped him see that man in Joshua, a man in whom the Spirit of God dwells. Joshua showed high potential in all the areas that Moses had in mind plus God-given talent, courage, and conviction that could be harnessed and mentored into being a great leader. He was already a good follower but needed to be a great leader.

Assess teachable habits

Assess teachable habits that will encourage the desired submission for growth. In addition to factors that are truly specific to different leadership responsibilities, the following factors are very common criteria in determining the servant leadership abilities of the potential successor:

(1) *Servanthood.* Servant-heart of leadership is the hallmark of great leaders and exposes pride in the followers; what motivates them to perform determines their effectiveness to be successors in servant leadership ministry.

(2) *Value system.* The value system begins with the thoughts that build the character and beliefs and who the leader can become. Your people's skills and value placed on followers will determine the relationships that they can build; who you are will determine who you can influence to attract them to follow you.

(3) *Humility.* A submissive and teachable spirit allows them to emulate and reproduce good leaders; potentials are taught to fill gaps, and humility enables them to assume that position.

(4) *Self-security.* Only secure leaders can stoop and expend themselves serving others as Jesus did; they must be able to share themselves and empower others to grow.

(5) *Preparation.* Only people who are committed and prepared to lead others are ready to meet the challenges of leadership. They 'respond to' rather 'react to' situations.

(6) *Experience.* Most potential beginning leaders lack the initial experience for the leadership assignment. Self-will, self-determination, and perseverance in their past challenges in life prepare them to extend themselves.

(7) *Capability.* The ability to think strategically and the ability to cast a vision determine what they can do; people follow leaders who know where they are going with the follower.

(8) *Courage with conviction.* Courage to overcome the initial challenges in unfamiliar territory is very critical for success. This was very important to God for Moses and Joshua to lead. Conviction in the principles behind the mission strengthens your courage to initiate actions.

Mentee commits to mentoring

Mentee accepts and commits to becoming like the mentor. The potential leader must accept and commit to the reproduction process. There are times when a leader naturally attracts good candidates who aspire to become like the leader; those who are motivated by a vision, strength of character, approachability, and an established relationship. Such candidates usually come with the convictions of the leader and aspire to be like him or are loyal to help him succeed in his leadership goals. We see this in the life of David. Several good warriors fought for David based on these factors and joined him in Ziklag. And, "all these men of war, who could keep ranks, came to Hebron with a loyal heart, to make David king over all Israel; and all the rest of Israel were of one mind to make David king"(1 Chronicles 12:38). David had a track record that they remembered— his trust in his God, his slaying of the giant Goliath, and his victory over the Philistines. These good warriors see themselves in David. David had to reproduce his leadership and heart in them. He also wanted these ordinary/good warriors to be great giant-killer warriors as he was. Only a giant killer can reproduce another giant killer. You simply grow into someone capable of transforming into what you have become. David accomplished this by three very simple natural acts that emanated from his own servant-heart attributes:

(1) **He modeled how to be adaptable.** David could recognize and adapt to changes in the environment and trigger changes accordingly to meet new requirements. He was also self-aware of what it would take to perform in the changed environment, even in the wilderness. To him, failure was not an option, and the wilderness environment was not an excuse for failing to succeed.
(2) **He modeled how to be humble and yet self-secured.** David gave up his right for the ultimate rewards and recognition of victory and the spoils from battle. He motivated his followers with words of affirmation and encouragement.

He modeled what he wanted them to become. David modeled a leadership style with clear examples and humility that the men wanted to emulate. David was the kind of general who the enemies feared. If that is not an attribute of a giant, I'm not sure what is!

SUMMARY 3
DEVELOPING THE ACTS OF REPRODUCTION-SELECTION

Before starting this exercise, please read and follow the instruction in the preface of this workbook. Answers to these questions are contained in this chapter. Completion of these exercises after reading the chapter should take 60-90 minutes.

Discovering the Acts of Reproduction-Selection

1. Define Reproduction–selection attitude. How important is Selection in reproduction attribute and what strategies are involved?
2. Identify the four-stage progression process model of servant leadership reproduction-attribute.
3. What did God see in Moses that made Him insist on convincing Moses to initiate the exodus of the Children of Israel out of Egypt? God wanted a patient diplomat who will be submissive to His leadership.

Practicing the Act of Reproduction-Selection Attribute

1. What can we learn from growth of followers: Joshua from Moses, Timothy from Paul, and Disciples from Jesus?
2. How do you Assess desired character and competency. What can we learn from Moses selecting Joshua as his successor (Numbers 27:17-23).
3. What eight factors were identified as very common criteria in determining the servant leadership abilities of the potential successor:
4. What is the role a mentee committing to the mentorship of the leader in a leadership reproduction process.

5. Compare with the life of David and his followers (1 Chronicles 12:38).), Jesus and his followers Moses and Joshua   How did David make ordinary/good warriors to be great giant-killer warriors as he was.

Reproduction-Selection is learning how to select a follower or leader to be trained to reproduce your leadership. It is the competence of a leader to select the right candidate to be developed as a successor.

1. How can selection be a means of modeling the attribute that your followers will want to emulate
2. What strategies can strengthen a mentor's competence for reproduction-selection:
3. What factors do you consider in determining the servant leadership abilities of the potential successor:

CHAPTER 4
DEVELOPING REPRODUCTION-MENTORING

Reproduction-mentoring is a process of achieving success through a relationship with an experienced facilitator. In reproduction–mentoring, a seasoned person duplicates himself in another less-experienced person; this is what I call a "mentee". Typically, a mentor provides guidance, facilitates the transition from one stage of life to a higher one (school to work, servant or follower to leader, child to adulthood, etc.), serves as a role model, counsels the men-tee on different topics of concern, and offers insights and perspective on the world.

The mentor is also open to discussing relationships or any topic of interest with the mentee. The mentors play the role of supporting, pushing, and influencing the men-tee to adopt the desired learning behaviors and the necessary experiences that will help realize his or her dream (ambition). Mentoring relationship changes over time as the mentor and men-tee grow, learn, and gain experience in the relationship. Effective mentoring that generates pronounced results requires time to produce oneself into another, to pass on one's dreams and visions to another, and to equip another person who may have a distinctive disposition, different gender, age, ethnicity, race, education, or spiritual level. Talent or gifts alone do not produce inordinate leadership but are the essential beginning point for becoming great.

The primary goal of leadership mentoring is to help train and transform good talent into great leadership by using a pronounced leader as the model of the identity and the "brain to pick." Formal mentoring involves matching a more experienced person, the mentor, with a less-experienced person, the mentee or protégé, and engaging them in a one-on-one relationship that is non-threatening and nonjudgmental but provides the challenge and pushes in the right direction.

Strategies for mentoring in different settings are well documented in the pieces of literature of academia, athletics, churches, corporations (profit and nonprofit), the military, and many others. In this instance, we focus on leader-servants. Gungy and Whitaker (2010) in their book, *The Mentor Leader* listed the essential traits of a mentor leader as [41] The Mentor leadership can be taught, learned, and practiced in order to be effective.

- Mentor leadership focuses on developing the strengths of the individuals by building specific skills.
- Mentors leaders who are successful make the people they mentor better in what they (the men-tees) do—students, players, workers, etc.
- Mentor leadership works best when the mentee is aware the mentor has a genuine interest in his or her development.

These traits can also be found as part of key strategies for effective mentoring of great leader-servants. Other strategies include the following:

Create reproduction mentoring–apprenticeship

In academic settings, faculty selects graduate students to mentor to become like or better than they are or who will do more than and represent them and their training in their chosen research field. A mentor is much more than an advisor. In science and engineering, for example, mentoring often takes the form of an apprenticeship relationship, including socializing the student to the norms of the field or the community to which the field belongs. The guidance is not as observable as teaching a laboratory technique. Instead, the benefits are largely intangible, with the faculty modeling thinking and problem-solving ability to the student. The relationships with mentors tend to be deeper and more personal even after graduate school; mentors are often a source of information and support until the men-tee becomes independent. The mentor's goals are to make "apprentice" or protégé to be a better replication of the mentor and to grow beyond the mentor.

Create hands-on-experience practices

Training for personal growth: Under the guidance of a mentor in this case Moses, the men-tee gained the needed hands-on experiences to deal with the issues at hand. Moses engaged Joshua and allowed him to share his life experiences—his courage, his fears, and the awesomeness of his responsibilities. He led him to see how to define problems and propose solutions, and how design and carry out the solutions. The end goal is to become an independent leader and even a greater leader with an expanded vision bigger than where they started.

Act of shepherding for immediate need. In Matthew 14:13-20 and John 6:1-18, Jesus directly involved his disciples in feeding the five thousand people with two fishes, five loaves of bread, and the miracle of several baskets over. Jesus gave his disciples hands-on experience through direct participation and observing the miracle. They gained first-hand experience in what it means to serve others in the ministry. The leader needs to be observant and understand the human conditions of the people they serve and be empathetic and compassionate. Leaders (Moses, Jeremiah, Isaiah, and David, etc.) are always inadequate for the task Jesus has for them in leadership. Paul reminded them of this fact "Not that we are sufficient in ourselves to claim anything as coming from us, but our sufficiency is from God..."2 Corinthians 3:5

Compassionate servants offer care for hurting sheep. They also learned that sympathetic servants are few. As with Moses leading the Children of Israel, sheep often outnumber the desired number of caregivers. We need to pray for more shepherds, which is what Jesus tells his disciples to do in; Matthew 9:37 "The harvest is plentiful, but the laborers are few" What is needed for the lost sheep is an increase in compassionate leaders who can offer more care. The disciples learned the leadership act of shepherding the sheep who may often feel helpless, hopeless, scared, and desperately in need. In picking up the pieces of 12 baskets, Jesus wanted the disciples to demonstrate on a practical level that God's provision was more than sufficient to meet the needs. Jesus is always more than adequate in every task and challenges we face.

Humility is a part of authentic leadership. The Leader-servants clean up after others while in his duty. Leaders pick up the mess as part of his role in servant leadership. Now Jesus commanded them to pick up after everyone. How easy and justified would it have been for these tired disciples to feel, "my job of distributing the food is over," or "It's not my job to clean up." This is one great lesson in humility in servant leadership. They had to clean up the mess they did not make.

Develop reproduction mentoring relationship

Develop reproduction mentoring relationship that reproduces. Imagine that your age difference is many years, your educational level is several degrees apart too; your academic rank or position in the company cannot be compared. You are thus the leader, and he or she desires to be like you, or you want him to replace you. How do you encourage someone to become like you or to be what he or she has never been before? From experience with these scenarios, the answer lies in the nature of the mentoring relationship. Here are a few strategies on mentor–relationship that reproduces leadership qualities with great wholeness:

Foster mentee-centered growth rather than goal-centered- An ability to communicate effectively is a key in the mentor–men-tee relationship. When goals and the mentoring purpose are not well communicated and understood, well-intentioned actions can be perceived as imperialism or even servitude.

Three critical elements:
(1) It creates and commits to a meaningful goal,
(2) It creates a plan to achieve that goal, and
(3) It continuously assesses the progress in attaining the goal.

The success of the mentoring process is measured by the level to which the goal was attained. My approach to mentoring students early in my career was more on pushing them to succeed or perform beyond their levels. I earned my education over 12 years at three universities. With four degrees in multiple fields, I was never taught by or saw a single black or female professor or had what I would call a good mentor. Yes, I had academic or research advisors, but I never had a person who believed in me and wanted me to be like or better than him. So my primary purpose as a mentor myself was very personal—preparing students, especially students traditionally under-represented in science and engineering—to graduate school and possibly for the professorate. There were times when my students felt I was pushing them too hard. In one particular case, I had an excellent student whom I thought could be whatever she wanted to be in my field or any other field of research. She was an undergraduate Physics junior. The project on which we were working was a graduate-level funded project. To me, the relationship was project-centered without much regard for the student's level. Yes, I led her to see what graduate school could be like and guided her to understand materials and how to analyze the data, but there was no effort to empathize with what she was feeling and her difficulties. The result was that she appreciated my pushing as she went on to complete her Ph.D.

A few years later, we ran into each other at a professional conference. After exchanging a few pleasantries, we sat down to catch up on lost time. I was happy to hear that she had completed her Ph.D; in fact, she was in one of my first sets of students to complete her Ph.D. As we sat down, our discussion went into mentoring and what it all means. She said, "Dr. Wosu, I want you to know that as far as the mentoring you provided to us; I truly appreciated all that you did for us. You motivated and instilled a desire for excellence in me. However, I wanted to let you know that you could have added to that push a little sensitivity, self-awareness, and student-centered relationship instead of being so project-centered." She said it jokingly, but I knew she was dead serious as I could read from the words she had not spoken written on her face. She said that she could not remember me ever appreciating or affirming her work. This student was broken, had carried this hurt, and had looked for a moment of healing. It was as if she had memorized what to tell me anytime she met me. I was glad she had at that moment, because it gave her the opportunity to express herself, the way she did. I admitted my omission. Accepting my lack of self-awareness not only brought healing to her but completely transformed my mentoring strategy. Speaking as a material scientist, I believe that you can bend a mentee to conform and rebound, but you cannot afford to bend him or her beyond the elastic limit to break him or her.

Respect, encourage, and affirm the mentee. Once a climate and culture of trust are established, affirming and encouraging your men-tee will enhance the opportunity to push the men-tee to high expectations. The men-tee must feel valued and assured the words of affirmation and encouragement are coming from a leader who has his or her interests in mind. Furthermore, the leader must be walking the talks and using words in the affirmation. It is damaging to one word to affirm an individual and curse the same individual for a minor error. The individual is more likely to remember or reflect on the negative word than on the positive. Never punish or reprimand a mentee for a mistake. For outright disobedience of well-communicated instruction, there has to be discipline but in the utmost respect of the individual and clear rejection of the action. The reprimand should be in form of discipline to improve rather than correction to punish.

Leaders should make an effort to take the men-tee out to conferences, excursions, and lunchtime in the company of others but focus on the mentee. In scheduled private meetings with the mentee, a mentor should share experiences and allow the men-tee to share in that experience such as an excellent game or movie you watched, the good fishing you went to, the latest encounter in your walk with God, the recent decision you made (the context, what you did and how you did it), etc. One of the most effective ways I have impacted students and colleagues were by sharing my unique stories—failures and successes. In failures, I shared what the failure or mistake was and how I made corrections to move past the failures. In success, I shared what made the success possible and credited all those that contributed to the success. Moses encouraged Joshua as much as possible in a climate of a good parent–son relationship for the immediate and future needs of Joshua to become a great leader.

Foster mentoring culture and climate

Foster mentoring culture and climate that establish trust for Reproduction. Effective mentoring thrives in a positive mentoring culture. What type of culture maximizes mentoring that reproduces great leaders? First, let us consider the definitions of culture. One definition of culture is "the action of developing the intellectual and moral faculties through education, the set of divided values and practices that characterizes an institution…"[42] Or "A shared, learned, symbolic system of values, beliefs, and attitudes that shapes and influences perception and behavior" [43] One can also define culture as "the shared knowledge and schemes created by a set of people for perceiving, interpreting, expressing, and responding to the social realities around them." [44] Second, with respect to Servant leadership, a mentoring culture reproduces a leader-servant as: a learned system of values and beliefs shared to shape and influence the servant leadership behavior. It can also be seen as a shared system patterned to impact the mentee's leadership skills while responding to the realities in which the mentee and mentor operate.

Develop reproduction-mentoring culture

Develop the reproduction-mentoring culture for servant leadership. Five key elements in our definition that are critical to effective mentoring culture it is:
(1) Learned to shape behavior,
(2) Patterned to impact leadership,
(3) Has core values and beliefs that empower,
(4) Has shared expectations to influence leadership, and
(5) Supports and responds to leadership realities.

Each of these elements is described below:

- *Mentoring culture is learned to shape* behaviors such as accountability, servanthood, ownership, intentionality, and roles to enhance function as well as feature consistent practices of effective goal-setting, formulating mentee-centered growth activities, and clarifying leadership expectations.
- *Mentoring culture is patterned to impact leadership.* The values, practices, mission, and goals of the mentor training and organization are aligned to reproduce the desired leadership–mentoring outcome and support activities that create and sustain the value and visibility of the mentee.
- *Mentoring culture has core values and* beliefs to empower reproducing leaders and is effectively shared and communicated to achieve mentoring excellence and positive results that increase trust, strengthen relationships, create servant leadership values, elevate the visibility of the men-tee, and model desired behaviors based on the leaders' own examples.
- *Mentoring culture has shared expectations to influence leadership.* The Mutual expectations and respect shared and understood between mentor, and men-tee will form the basis of rewards and recognition.
- *Mentoring culture supports and responds to realities* in the environment. Multiple mentoring approaches are available to create a culture that advances; supports, and models desired skills.

Lois J. Zachary writing about the culture of managing people as a human factor in Human Resources suggests that a mentoring culture must "continuously focus on building the mentoring capacity, competence, and capability of the organization." [45]

Develop reproduction-mentoring climate

Develop a reproduction-mentoring climate for servant leadership. Even in the presence of a positive mentoring culture, the success of the mentoring program depends largely on the support of a beneficial environmental climate. I will define mentoring climate as the perceived or dominant condition (attitudes, behaviors, approachability, and standards) in the mentoring situation or the organizational setup with respect to the mentee–mentor relationship, mentoring culture, receptivity, and sensitivity to individual differences. It also refers to the general perception of the mentor and mentor of the mentoring relationship. The quality of the beneficial mentoring climate can be measured by things such as the level of positive attitudes toward racial and gender differences, the level of sense of belonging to the relationship, and the evidence of t mutual respect that permeates the culture, regardless of diversity. "An advantageous climate is one in which favorable feelings and interpretations predominate over negative feelings and interpretations." [46] This leads to explicit emotions and optimal mentor -men-tee engagement in the relationship. Since a leader's personality has a profound impact on the mentoring climate, effective mentoring depends on the practical personality of the mentor who is expected according to research to induce, develop, and display positive emotions in the mentee. The climate affects the mentee's interpretation of their circumstances and communication with the mentor. A Positive mentoring climate focuses on inducing beneficial emotions, which have been shown to enlarge a cognitive perspective that enhances the ability of the men-tee to make richer interpretations and experience growth and productivity.

Summary 4
Developing Reproduction-Mentoring

Before starting this exercise, please read and follow the instruction in the preface of this workbook. Answers to these questions are contained in this chapter. Completion of these exercises after reading the chapter should take 60-90 minutes.

Discovering the Acts of Reproduction-Mentoring

1. What is reproduction-mentoring? Describe a time you have been mentored by someone; what was the purpose and outcome of the relationship?
2. Define a mentor and the role of mentor in a mentor-mentee relationship
3. What is the primary goal of leadership mentoring
4. What are essential traits of a mentor leader?

Principle

Reproduction-Mentoring is learning the process of achieving success through a relationship with an experienced facilitator.

1. How can an experienced person reproduce himself in another less experienced person here called a mentee?
2. List three strategies for effective mentoring of a great leaders

Practicing acts of Reproduction-mentoring

1. One of the strategies discussed for mentoring was to create reproduction mentoring–apprenticeship. How does this work best in academic setting?
2. How can a mentor create hands-on-experience practices for mentee
3. What did Jesus teach about the Act of shepherding for immediate need of followers (Matthew 14:13-20 and John 6:1-18)
4. Case example: Developing reproduction mentoring relationship. Imagine that your age difference is many years, your educational level is several degrees apart too; your

academic rank or position in the company cannot be compared. You are thus the leader, and he or she desires to be like you, or you want him to replace you.
   a. How do you encourage someone to become like you or to be what he or she has never been before?
   b. What are some strategies in this mentor–relationship that reproduces leadership qualities desired?
   c. How do you measure the success of the mentoring process?
5. **Foster mentoring culture and climate requires leader to** Foster mentoring culture and climate that establish trust for Reproduction. What type of culture maximizes mentoring that reproduces great leaders?
6. What are the Five key elements critical to effective mentoring culture
7. Even in the presence of a positive mentoring culture, the success of the mentoring program depends largely on the support of a beneficial environmental climate. How do you define such mentoring climate How does the climate affects the mentee's interpretation of their circumstances and communication with the mentor.

Mentoring-Relationship is developed to encourage someone to become like you or to be what he or she has never been before from experience in these scenarios, the answer lies in the nature of the mentoring relationship:
1. What is Mentoring-Culture and how does it impact the relationship
2. What are the five key elements of an effective mentoring culture?
3. What is Mentoring-Empowerment with for reproduction attribute?

CHAPTER 5
DEVELOPING REPRODUCTION-EQUIPPING

The reproduction–equipping is the leader's acts of training and equipping the men-tee for independence in the present and future work of the ministry. Ministries change from time to time. Leaders expand their vision for a higher calling. Reproduction means very little as far as a legacy is concerned unless the mentee reaches the point of independence and can stand on his or her own feet. This goal is accomplished by carefully equipping the follower.

Equip the followers for independence

It takes several years to release a newborn to be independent. In the same way, a young believer also needs attentive nurturing to grow into independence. Paul carefully addressed this in; "For though by this time, you ought to be teachers, you need someone to teach you again the basic principles of the oracles of God. You need milk, not solid food." Hebrews 5:12: Attentive discipleship is needed to treat each person as unique by him- or herself. Paul, in addressing the Ephesus elders, told them: "Watch out! Remember the three years I was with you—my constant watch and care over you night and day, and my many tears for you" (Acts 20:31).

Equip the followers with sound doctrine

Equip the followers with sound doctrine in which you believe. Imagine planting a new church and a new vision for growth in a new city or neighborhood. The new church is to start with fresh Christians and potential leaders. You have the vision and know exactly what is needed for this new ministry. However, you cannot be in two places at the same time. How do you reproduce yourself, your vision, and your leadership? This was the situation Paul faced when he planted a church in Thessalonica with the converted Christians, who had committed with the conviction to follow Jesus. Nevertheless, they needed leadership training—Paul's type of leadership. Paul's letters to Timothy (1 and 2

Timothy) have been considered by many as a leadership training manual. Timothy was one of the first fruits of Paul's ministry in spreading the Gospel of Christ and growing the church through increased conversion. Paul referred to Timothy as his son because he saw Timothy in him. Paul needed to train Timothy; however, more so that he could train trainers and leaders. Paul's training of Timothy focused on identifying and equipping others to help him grow the church by training more leaders.

What can we learn from Paul's example or his training manual? In 1 Timothy 4:12, he asked Timothy to be an example in words and teaching sound doctrine; be an example in conversation (in domestic and public); be an example in showing love-based service to others; be an example in the way all things are done, be an example in exercising faith in God, and be an example in purity. Here are more strategies we can list from Paul's writings. Of course, this list is not exhaustive but is a place to start:

Equip with appropriate discipline

Equip the followers by guiding followers to discipline the body. Jesus returned to His disciples and found them sleeping. He said; "Could you not keep watch for one hour? Watch and pray so that you will not fall into temptation. The spirit is willing but the body is weak" (Mark 14:37-38, NIV. In his book, The Character of God's Workman, Watchman Nee argues that God's workman must "discipline the body." [47] Jesus continued to challenge His followers as a way of empowering them. While He empathized with their human frailties, He wanted them to see the need to discipline their physical and spiritual bodies. Despite Peter's failures in that regard, with Jesus's encouragement, Peter grew up as one of the greatest of the disciples by following Jesus' examples. To better guide your followers, you just need to be in their lives to know them more and be able to empathize with them. As an example, Jesus saw that the body and the spirit were not of the same strength. The body is weak because they were tied yet the spirit was willing to sacrifice to follow and serve. Our responsibility as leaders is to guide the follower by enabling him to see why he needs to discipline the body and put it under the control of the inner spirit so that the weak body does not fall into temptation. They must start first by being watchful and vigilant because of the danger of temptations around and second, they must be fervent in prayer for support from God.

Equip with encouragement and enablement

Equip others by providing encouragement and enablement for independence. The Enablements for independence are such things as resources, information, specific training, and empowerment that provide the capacity for the reproductive growth of the follower. The mentor shares information and power with the men-tee to build his or her capacity to take initiative and decisions to solve problems and improve service and performance when released to service. The mentor is totally committed to nurturing and encouraging the men-tee, inspiring the growth in him that he desires As a leader-servant, the mentor readily gives power to others (Rom 5:12-21), including skills, resources, authority, opportunity, and motivation, as well as holding others responsible and accountable for the outcomes of their actions. Strategies for quipping by encouragement and enablement for independence include:

Communicate a good plan with a personal touch. Jesus throughout his ministry communicated a clear, precise, and detailed plan based on an understandable vision of what He wanted the disciples to do and why. The Apostle Paul in encouraging Timothy and Titus also personally communicated a good plan and pattern that they must observe from his individual example of following Jesus. An excellent leader cannot send his followers on a mission that represents his success or failure without a clear plan, just as if he is right there carrying on the mission. A leader must also communicate personal care with self-awareness of the challenges ahead and should use whatever means to build strength and independence in the follower. Here are Jesus's words when he sent forward the disciples: "And He called the twelve to Himself, and began to send them out two by two, and gave them power over unclean spirits..." (Mark 6: 7-9, NKJV). This is a powerful statement of care and power over filthy spirits. Jesus called out as a group but sent them out two by two.

Grow leaders and followers into the vision. Have you ever called your followers, colleagues, or your graduate students to join you in your vision as leaders? In reproduction, the men-tee usually does not quite know the mentor's vision. There are situations in which the leader or follower in another field or vision may be called to join a different vision or department. How do you as a leader equip and grow potential leaders or followers into your vision which you desire them to follow? How did Jesus develop His disciples into His vision? Or how did Paul develop Timothy into seeing his vision? Here are a few examples:

Call followers to join in the vision as leaders. The effort to introduce and reproduce your new vision into the group will usually differ from selecting a candidate men-tee. In this case, you select a potential leader and grow him or her into the vision. We can see a few examples of these points in the lives of Jesus, Paul, Timothy, and others. At the beginning of Jesus' ministry, He knew that the vision would take several leaders to accomplish. He also knew that the uniqueness of the ministry would mean reproducing Himself in others: He called other leaders by naming disciples to join Him (Matthew 4:18-22). He began developing them into future leader-servants for the church. First, He chose three fishermen. These men were good at fishing but; "He said to them, "Follow Me", and I will make you fishers of men" (Matthew 4:19, NKJV). They were leaders in their field of fishing. They knew where and how to fish for fish in different sea environments. They met His requirements and conviction in what they believed. However, they needed more than conviction in this arena to which Jesus was calling them. So, to their conviction and attitude of hard work, Jesus added a new vision of spiritual reproduction. He desired them to be fishers of men. To their fishing abilities, he spoke the language they would understand—a "fisher" of men, a clear, higher, and different calling of leadership.

Who would you consider replicating youself? Where and how do you find those candidates? How do you select them? We can answer these questions from Jesus' examples;

- Look and find followers from your daily work of life as potential leaders.
- Select the potential leader with conviction and the right match for the purpose.
- Communicate the vision to them, so they become leaders of influence.
- Make the vision clearer in the language they understand.
- Inspire them to follow a greater course—fish men instead of fish.

Demonstrate your zeal and leadership plus a personal passion for the vision. Jesus modeled leadership to them as he traveled through Judea.

SUMMARY 5
DEVELOPING REPRODUCTION-EQUIPPING

Before starting this exercise, please read and follow the instruction in the preface of this workbook. Answers to these questions are contained in this chapter. Completion of these exercises after reading the chapter should take 60-90 minutes.

Discovering the Acts of Reproduction-Equipping

1. What is reproduction–equipping? What is the role of equipping the mentee in reproducing leadership qualities?
2. What exactly you to equip the followers for? What does Paul teach about equipping in Hebrews 5:12:" (Acts 20:31).
3. Paul's letters to Timothy (1 and 2 Timothy) have been considered by many as a leadership training manual. What can we learn from Paul's example or his training manual on how to equip followers?. what did Paul train—character or skills?

Understanding the principle of Reproduction-equipping

Equipping is gaining the ability to train and equip the mentee for independence in the present and future work of the ministry.
1. How can leaders expand their vision for a higher calling?
2. How can leaders equip their followers with sound doctrine

Practicing the Acts of Reproduction equipping

1. What are some of proper disciplines that need to be equipped and how?
2. How do you equip a follower with encouragement and enablement?
3. Who would you consider replicating yourself? Where and how do you find those candidates? How do you select them? How did Jesus answer these questions from His examples;

CHAPTER 6
DEVELOPING REPRODUCTION-RELEASING

Reproduction–releasing is the leader's act of releasing and trusting the trainees to demonstrate leadership and train others (Luke 24:46-49). This is the only way to allow trainees to continue developing the vision. The "Great Commission" was Jesus' example of releasing the disciples after reproducing Christ-like vision and Servanthood in them. Several lessons can be learned from how Jesus released His disciples to reproduce His leadership in carrying out the vision of His ministry, including the following:

(1) He communicated the vision and mission. Jesus trained and sent out the disciples with the foresight of a visionary leader. He said; "It's still four months until harvest?" I tell you, open your eyes and look at the fields! They are ripe for harvest" (John 4:35). He also sent them with understanding. Vision–Measure and learn how to assess what matters; for the most part. When the 70 He sent out returned with joy with the excitement that the demons were subject to them in the name of Jesus, He told them they should rejoice that their names were written in heaven instead; "blessed are the eyes which see the things you see"(Luke 10:17-24, NKJV).

(2) He inspired in them the heart of service. Jesus expended Himself on the 12 Apostles and showed them. His acts of Servanthood. When the 70 returned from the mission, they reported that the sick were healed, lepers were cleansed, the dead were raised, and the devil was cast out (Matthew 10:3).

(3) He was assured of their commitment and sacrifice to the mission. He made sure they were fully committed and willing to make the needed sacrifice to follow Him, "If anyone desires to come after Me, let him deny himself, and take up his cross, and follow Me" (Matthew 16:24).

(4) He created an opportunity for personal connection. Jesus was very intimate and close with the disciples, who added to their confidence as He separated them into smaller groups. "And He

called the twelve to Himself, and began to send them out two by two, and gave them power over unclean spirits" (Mark 6:7).

(5) He communicated the vision–mandate. Jesus reassured them of His leadership presence with them. He sent with a clear command to reflect the integrity and seriousness of their training and the purpose of the mission without compromise and in reverence, giving glory only to God.

(6) The Vision-means: He shared privileged information. As part of His transparency in dealing with this inner cycle, of leaders, Jesus made it a point to share very freely with them, preparing them with information about Him, His relationship with His Father, His concerns about the ministry, and so on—information that He could not share with any other. He said; "To you, it has been given to know the mysteries of the kingdom of God, but to the rest, it is given in parables, that 'Seeing they may not see, and hearing they may not understand" (Luke 8:9, 10).

(7) The Vision Model: He communicated the model to follow. Jesus fully demonstrated Servant Leadership through His example in preparing them for service. "For I have given you an example that you should do as I have done to you" (John 13:15). "Now it came to pass, afterward, that He went through every city and village, preaching and bringing the glad tidings of the kingdom of God. And the twelve were with Him" (Luke 8:1). By this, Jesus allowed them to learn directly from Him to equip them as He was preparing to send them out on a similar mission. "Then He appointed twelve, that they might be with Him and that He might send them out to preach" (Mark 3:14).

(8) He maintained a close relationship with them. It was not enough to call them and train them for the ministry. He maintained good relationships with them as He sent them out and revealed to them what they needed to be effective. "No longer do I call you servants, for a servant, does not know what his master is doing; however, I have called you friends, for all things that I heard from My Father; I have made known to you" (John 15:15). He demonstrated his friendship till the end; "Having loved His own who were in the world, He loved them to the end" (John 13:1).

(9) Vision-Method: He empowered them to achieve greater things. As a vision method, power in Jesus was the tool on which they must

CHAPTER 6
DEVELOPING REPRODUCTION-RELEASING

depend. Jesus described the territory into which the disciples were stepping. He had been there and knew that Devil would stand against them to steal, kill and destroy the work. So, it was important to send them out with full power and backing; "Overall the power of the enemy and nothing shall by any means hurt you" (Luke 10:19, NKJV). His last words to them were: "But you shall receive power when the Holy Spirit has come upon you, and you shall be witnesses to Me... to the end of the earth" (Acts 1:8, NKJV).

He sent them with Trust–Confidence. Out of the many disciples after Him, Jesus selected 12 with whom he spent a lot of time training and preparing for ministry. "And when it was day, He called His disciples to Himself; and from them, He chose twelve whom He also named apostles" (Luke 6:12-13, NKJV) The name Apostle means that they are to stand as promoters or supporters of His ministries. He demonstrated trust in them to build their confidence in the significance of the calling. He also assured them that He was sending them as the Father had sent Him. Comparing the Father's trust condolence to His is a profound and inspiring expression of the trust He had in them. Think about a King you respect, and this King has a high external positive reputation. The King comes to you, saying, "I have selected you to attend a meeting to represent me—my vision, my message, my personality." How will you feel? Of course, you will be inspired, humbled, and trusted. Only a King who trusts you will send you on an important mission as his promoter.

Publicly commission the mentee

Jesus publicly portrayed His disciples as leaders and lobbied for them to gain open recognition and respect. Moses openly recognized Joshua's leadership by laying hands on him and overtly commissioning him. He gave Joshua part of his authority (Numbers. 27: 15-23). Joshua received positive recognition, the leader's approval and acceptance, and Moses' expression of faith in him.

Release followers with encouragement to be courageous

Jesus sent out His twelve disciples to serve as sheep in the midst of wolves. Jesus said:

Behold, I send you out as sheep in the midst of wolves. Therefore be wise as serpents and harmless as doves...But when they deliver you up, do not worry about how or what you should speak. For it will be given to you in that hour what you should speak; for it is not you who speak, but the Spirit of your Father who speaks in you...A disciple is not above his teacher, nor a servant above his master. It is enough for a disciple that he be like his teacher, and a servant like his master... Therefore do not fear them" (Matthew 10:16-25).

He prepared them for the mission by reminding them that what they need will be given to them. This implies that He will be reproducing Himself in them. He reminds them that it will be enough for them to just be like Him—His own leadership and power will be in them. In preparing his disciples, He communicated and instructed them about what they should expect as sheep in the midst of wolves. His instructions were clear and specific:

- *Be courageous, wise, and innocent.* He instructed them of possible opposition; opposition to the gospel, religious men, and rulers. There will be wolves (danger), but be wise (serpent), but innocent (dove).
- *Be prepared for hardship.* This communicates and prepares them about future hardships and instructs them on how to handle these hardships.
- *Be confident of victory.* Jesus predicts their personal anguish but gives them hope and assurance of ultimate victory.
- *Be emulators of the master* but submit to the authority of the master
- *Trust in God* because He that sent you will be with you and meet your needs.
- *Be what I have been to you.* Trainees must recognize that trainers can reproduce only what they are.

Release the following by preparing for rejection

No follower can fully represent his mentor 100% or the leader in his ideas, vision, and method. The vision is born by the leader and transferred to the follower. So, no matter the training, executing a vision is usually best with the passion of the dreamer. Although Martin

Luther King, Jr. had many followers, none could completely reproduce him, even his speeches with the same passion with which he delivered them. The leader must therefore prepare his followers for possible rejection and hardships.

Jesus, in preparing to release his disciples, pointed out the possibility of some people not receiving or hearing them but prepared them with how they could respond. In the process, Jesus was authoritative, reassuring, and pragmatic. First, He was very personal; indeed, He called them to Himself. He warned them of possible rejection and to be prepared for it rather than be paralyzed with fear and discouragement when it occurs. He was not making any conditional statements but almost telling than that rejection would surely occur. He prepared them mentally and emotionally for it. Leaders preparing for their reproduction must empower followers by increasing their resilience to face rejection. Jesus himself was rejected by many, even His own people. So, He prepared them to equip their minds to learn to move to pass any opposition and persecution.

1. Guard the true doctrine by refusing speculative doctrine.
2. Be dependable to your calling through faith and conviction
3. Be a model that others can follow by pattering what you want others to be.
4. Be diligent in carrying out the duties assigned to you.
5. Create opportunities to teach followers what they need to prepare for growth.
6. Lead others more by "walking the talk" than talking the walk.
7. Define your legacy and lead by example to empower others to pass it on.
8. Be engaged with your new leaders and continue to advance their development through frequent encouragement, affirmations, and feedback.
9. Be reproductive as a teacher and submissive as a servant
10. Correct in error, prepare those who were called, and discipline in love.

Pass on the legacy to continue the vision

Your legacy is that part of your asset (gift, inheritance, heritage, vision) that you want to remain or continue after you are gone. It is part of your leadership accomplishments that you want to be passed on from generation to generation and for which you will be remembered.

Jesus was with His disciples for more than three years. He knew that a time would come when He would leave them and the ministry. The ministry of salvation and the church birth at that time was a significant legacy to Him. The work was important to God the Father and must continue even if others would come after Him. In the Great Commission, Jesus was passing on His legacy, the Gospel, which is to be preached to all nations, beginning from wherever you are. The writings of the disciples in the Gospels demonstrate that they actually understood the vision–message. Through the three and half years, His internal purpose was to prepare and equip these leaders by letting them see him "walk the talk" and as leaders reproduce the experience in others; they were sent to continue Jesus' work everywhere; "even to the uttermost part of the earth" (Acts 1:8, NKJV). By being ordinary people—fishermen and tax collectors, gentiles, and Jews, He taught them that anyone with a basic conviction can be trained to lead.

The future of the church was trusted on these disciples to build His church and a lasting legacy against which the; "gates of hell cannot prevail" (Matthew 16:18, NKJV). This was one reason Jesus saw the need to invest time in the "rock" Simon Peter to recover from his initial failures in denying Jesus three times. It was as if Peter had set aside everything he learned from Jesus. Nevertheless, Peter that repented and recovered was more convicted, more bold, and more resilient than ever before, in order to take his position of leadership.

Many have argued why Jesus Christ asked Peter three times if he loved Him to which Peter answered three times; "Yea, Lord; thou knowest that I love thee" (John 21:16, KJV) and to which the Lord responded; "Feed my sheep" (John 21:16, KJV).

This fisherman Peter was called to be a fisher of men was now charged to feed the sheep and be the rock on which the legacy stands to pass on. I believe Jesus asked Peter the question three times to emphasize the fact that the legacy must be passed based on a leader-servant that is motivated by love to serve others just as the Father sent Jesus to save the lost sheep of Israel and die for it because of love. Jesus made His legacy and was now ready to depend on Peter and the other disciples who were replications of Himself over the three years of His ministry. He was also encouraging and restoring Peter, who earlier had denied Him. Peter and the others knew that they must not be remembered, and without a successor, a leader fails to reproduce.

SUMMARY 6
DEVELOPING REPRODUCTION-RELEASING

Before starting this exercise, please read and follow the instruction in the preface of this workbook. Answers to these questions are contained in this chapter. Completion of these exercises after reading the chapter should take 60-90 minutes

What is Reproduction–releasing others?

1. The "Great Commission" was Jesus' example of releasing the disciples after reproducing Christ-like vision and Servanthood in them. What lessons were learned from how Jesus release of His disciples to reproduce His leadership in carrying out the vision of His ministry ((John 4:35).(Luke 10:17-24, NKJV); (Matthew 16:24; Mark 6:7).

Practicing the act of Reproduction-releasing

Reproduction-releasing is learning to release and trust the trainees to demonstrate leadership and train others. This is an essential way to allow him to carry on developing the vision.

1. What lessons can we learn from how Jesus released his disciples to reproduce His leadership? Take the Leadership Reproduction attribute audit in Table 8..
2. Based on the questions in Table 8.1, can you identify each of the acts of responsibility leadership attribute? What ones did you score 3 ("sometimes") or less than 3? Review and learn and commit to work to improve.

| \multicolumn{6}{c}{**Table 8.1. Leadership Reproduction Attribute Audit**} |

	Table 8.1. Leadership Reproduction Attribute Audit					
\multicolumn{7}{l}{*Servant leadership reproduction attribute is the combined acts of developing leadership qualities in others and releasing them as successors to continue a greater mission.* Assess the quality of your acts of reproduction attribute by inserting an X below the number that best describes your response to each statement.}
Item	Acts of Reproduction Attribute Check 1= Always; 2= Frequently; 3= Sometimes; 4= Almost; 5= Never	1	2	3	4	5
1	I am able to select the right candidate to be trained to reproduce what is desired.					
2	In selection, I assess teachable habits for desired submission for growth					
3	I select the people with the desired character to develop					
4	I act in ways to develop my leadership qualities in others					
5	I inspire success in others through building mutual respect and positive relationship.					
6	I empower and release my trained followers to be successors to continue a greater mission					
7	I assess and train desired character and competency that are need for the service					
8	I encourage growth in others through positive influence					
9	I foster mentoring culture and climate that establish trust for reproduction of a purpose					
10	I foster a culture of follower-centered growth rather than goal-centered					
11	**Add up your rating in each column**					
Score Range	Guide and Explanation of Score. understand the areas you need to further develop			Score		
10-17	Great Reproduction Leadership; keep it up!					
18-25	Above Average reproduction; need to work on 25% of the areas					
26-33	Average but developing ; need to work on 50% of the areas					
34-41	Below average reproduction; need to work on 75% of the areas					
42-50	No reproduction leadership ; work in all the areas					

CHAPTER 6
DEVELOPING REPRODUCTION-RELEASING

Case of release of the 70.

Jesus released His twelve disciples to serve as sheep in the midst of wolves. Jesus said:

> *Behold, I send you out as sheep in the midst of wolves. Therefore be wise as serpents and harmless as doves...But when they deliver you up, do not worry about how or what you should speak. For it will be given to you in that hour what you should speak; for it is not you who speak, but the Spirit of your Father who speaks in you....A disciple is not above his teacher, nor a servant above his master. It is enough for a disciple that he be like his teacher, and a servant like his master... Therefore do not fear them" (Matthew 10:16-25).*

1. What strategies did er follow what were the six elements of His instruction .
2. **How did he prepare his disciples in the case before he released them**
3. Your legacy is that part of your asset (gift, inheritance, heritage, vision) that you want to remain or continue after you are gone. How did Jesus **Pass on the legacy to continue the vision**
4. How did the disciples respond to Jesus

Topic Index

About This Book, 20
Affective Compassion, 77
authentic, 22, 24
authentic leadership, 35, 69
Authentic Leadership, 43
Authenticity, 41
Characteristics of Servant Leadership:
    Persuasion Attribute, 55
Comfort, 39
commitment, 17, 23
Comparisons
    with other works, 38
credibility, 46
Discipleship
    definition of, 25
distinguishes
    a leader's act of giving, 27
Functional Definitions, 33
Generosity
    definition of, 27
Generosity c, 27
giving, 27
    habit of, 27
Growing Leaders, 79
inside-out, 44
Jesus release of His disciples, 83, 89
Joshua, 17
law of, 40

Leader as Servant Leadership, 40
    definition, 23
Leader First., 21
Leader-as-Servant Leadership, 21
leader-servant's affection-attribute
    definition, 46
leadership, 23
Leadership Attributes, 41
Leadership Inner Value system, 23
Mentoring-Culture and Climate, 90
Model, 21
Moses, 17
Navigation-attribute, 46
Organizational leadership trust, 30
Pass on the legacy
    to reproduce yourself, 87, 91
Personal Outward Authenticity, 45
Practicing Servant Leadership
    Reproduction, 57
process, 23
Reproduction –selection, 64
Servant, 21, 22
test
    for leader-servant authenticity, 44
    of essential elements of personal
        authenticity, 44, 45
The Leadership Influence-attribute, 39

REFERENCES

[1]Greenleaf, R. (1970). *The Servant as Leader,* Indianapolis: The Robert K. Greenleaf Center

[2]Spears, L. (1996). *"Reflections on Robert K. Greenleaf and servant-leadership."* Leadership & Organization Development Journal, 17(7), 33-35

[3]Russell, R.F. (2001). "The role of values in servant leadership." *Leadership & Organization Development Journal,* 22(2), 76-83

[4]Russell, R.F., and Stone, A.G. (2002). "A review of servant leadership attributes: developing a practical model." *Leadership & Organization Development Journal,* 23(3), 145-15

[5]Terry. R. W (1993). *Authentic Leadership: Courage In Action,* San Francisco, CA ,Jossey-Bass

[6]George, B (2003). *Authentic Leadership: Rediscovering the Secrets to Creating Lasting Value.* San Francisco, CA, Jossey-Bass

[7]Shamir, B. & Eilam, G. (2005). "What's your story? Toward a life-story approach to authentic leadership." Leadership Quarterly, 16, 395–418.

[8]Anderson, GL (2009). Advocacy Leadership: Toward a Post-Reform Agenda in Education, Routledge, New York, 41

[9]Yacobi, B.G. *"Elements of Human Authenticity."* http://www.philosophytogo.org /wordpress/?p=1945, Retrieved, July 15, 2012

[10]George, B (2003). *Authentic Leadership: Rediscovering the Secrets to Creating Lasting Value,* San Francisco, CA, Jossey-Bass

[11]Wosu, SN (2014), *Leader as Servant Leadership Model,* Xulon Press

[40]Maxwell, JC (2005). *The 360-Degree Leader,* Published by Thomas Nelson, Inc.

[41]Dungy, T and Whitaker, N (2010). *The Mentor Leader,* Tyndale Housing Publishing, Inc.

[42](Merriam-Webster, 2008

[43]Dahl, K. (2007). Eastern Oregon University, LaGrande, OR.

[44] Lederach, J.P. (1995). Preparing for peace: Conflict transformation across cultures. Syracuse, NY: Syracuse University Press, p. 9

[45] Zachary, L. J. "How to Create a Mentoring Culture: Hallmarks of a Mentoring Culture" http://humanresources.about.com/od/coachingmentoring/a/mentor_culture.htm. Retrieved

[46] Cameron, K.S., & Caza, A. (2005). *Developing strategies for responsible leadership.* In J. Doh & S. Stumph (Eds.), Handbook on responsible leadership and governance in global business

[47] Nee, Watchman (1988). *The Character of God's Workman*, Christian Fellowship Publisher, NY

www.ingramcontent.com/pod-product-compliance
Lightning Source LLC
LaVergne TN
LVHW061556070526
838199LV00077B/7078